CELTIC SKELET

AN ENGLISHMAN'S JOURNEY INTO HIS
WELSH, CORNISH AND SCOTTISH ANCESTRY

CELTIC SKELETONS

An Englishman's journey
into his
Welsh, Cornish and Scottish ancestry

by
TONY BERRY

First published 2019

Copyright ©Tony Berry 2019

Highshore Publications.
13 Highshore House, New Bridge Street,
Truro, Cornwall, UK, TR12FE

www.yarraboy.com

Tony Berry is a journalist, editor and writer of crime fiction who has worked on newspapers, journals and magazines in the UK and Australia, where he emigrated several decades ago. In 2010 he made a spur of the moment decision to return to the UK and set up base in Cornwall while researching his family history. This resulted in the publication in 2011 of *From Paupers to iPads*, the story of his family across seven generations and three continents.

He continues to edit fiction and non-fiction for clients in Australia and the UK and served for several years as editor of the quarterly journal of the Cornwall Family History Society. He devotes much of his spare time to running and for several years has been recognised as an elite competitor in masters' athletics at national and international level for distances from 5000m to the full marathon.

His first two crime novels were shortlisted for the New South Wales Genre Fiction Award and the second also secured him one of only seven mentorships awarded by the Australian Society of Authors. He has since completed three more books in the ongoing series.

Tony is a member of the Australian Society of Authors and a fully accredited member of the Institute of Professional Editors (Australia) and the Society of Editors and Proofreaders (UK).

Dedicated to all my ancestors and forebears in honour of the hard lives so many of them endured and with apologies for any distortions, inaccuracies, aspersions that may have been unwittingly and unintentionally cast upon them in creating this admittedly fanciful story of their lives. All corrections, amendments and adjustments will be gratefully received and acknowledged.

Deepest thanks, too, to the many co-researchers, family historians and hitherto unknown relatives who have provided help and information. Despite the risk of inadvertently omitting much appreciated contributors, mention must be made of the invaluable input provided by Lynne Tasker (who set me off on this journey), Heather Williams, Amanda Jones, Bob Richardson, Sylvia Allen, June Topping, Sally Pocock, Judy Mansell, Donna Kopnick, Gillian Glover, Margaret Dimech, Sharon Stephens, Sylvia Allen, Sylvia Druett, Jennifer Brinker, Al Kuehl, Sue Moore, SW Poon, Steve Marshall, Kathryn Baird, Helen Hartley and no doubt several others encountered on the long, long trail that goes a-winding wherever family historians decide to set foot.

There has, of course, been much use of such excellent resources as Ancestry, Find My Past, FreeBMD, Family Search, Find A Grave, The National Archives, Cornwall Online Parish Clerks, Trinity House, the Commonwealth War Graves Commission, Cornwall's War History, Hong Kong Government Reports Online, Trove, workhouses.org.uk, the British Newspaper Archive, the Cornwall Records Office, Pembrokeshire Records Office, National Library of Wales and numerous other archives here and around the world.

All have played a vital part in making this book possible.

Pictures are largely of my own creation or have been sourced from ageing family albums (hence their often faded and blurred condition) or are licensed under Creative Commons. All attempts have been made to honour copyright and acknowledgement is made where required.

**Some chapters that follow contain material that appeared in From Paupers to iPads. It has, however, been updated and revised as a result of additional research undertaken in the intervening years. It is included to explain the many new connections that have been made and thus clarify the overall story of my Celtic journey and the ancestors encountered along the way.

CONTENTS

FOREWORD

THERE IS A WIDELY-HELD belief that journalists abide by a rule that states, 'never let the facts spoil a good story'. Having worked as a newspaper scribe for more than fifty years, it is an allegation I strongly deny.

Facts are paramount. Strenuous efforts are always made to verify them – despite the obstacles provided by those who prefer their own distorted and warped version of events. It is in the handling of the facts where things so often go awry, resulting in the slurs cast against well-intentioned reporters. The hows, whys and wherefores behind the facts are where interpretation so often varies.

The following work proves facts can be used in whatever way the writer chooses and I cheerfully confess to at times having played fast and loose with the information at hand. This is not because of any desire to put some fanciful personal spin on the past but because, as I have frequently found, the 'facts' with which family historians work are often far from as reliable as they are presented to be.

One of the largest online resources used by researchers is riddled with glaring errors. Some are caused by sub-standard transcriptions of old documents. Others are due to other researchers making wild assumptions and not only distorting their own family trees but then leaving their unsourced 'facts' for others to copy and thus perpetuate the errors. It is not unusual to find someone's distant relative supposedly being married well before the date of their birth, or children being born ahead of their parents. Such glaring errors are presented as unsourced 'facts' to be negligently repeated by unthinking fellow researchers who copy data without considering the logic of what they are adding to their family tree.

Another data disaster in the 'bleedingly obvious' category is exemplified in census details for a family living way down south in Plymouth, Devon, being headlined as the Census for Scotland 1861. Or locations in Britain being hijacked and relocated in the US by researchers clicking before pausing to check.

To have even the most laughably wrong entries corrected is nigh impossible. Most sites claim to provide a system for advising of errors. But that is as far as it gets as there is rarely any follow-up or amendment and the mistakes remain to be recycled ad nauseam.

Thus, the although the dates, names and places presented in this history have all been researched and documented, I can make no cast iron promise as to their veracity. And, as with all data rooted in the distant past, the events surrounding these facts are open to interpretation, as are many of the handwritten records from which they have been extracted.

Like most family researchers I came too late to my task. I began delving into the past long after my ancestors had passed on. All that remain are dates and names and often questionable records. The voices that could relate stories of family life, explain events and justify decisions fell silent decades ago. No one is there to whisper of the secret liaisons, the footloose husbands (and wives), the illegitimate children, the break-ups and divorces, and the errant offspring and spouses who simply, and deliberately, disappeared.

Three generations: the author (foreground) with his parents and grandparents in Gillingham in 1938

It was thus left to me to weave my own stories; to embroider the facts in order to enliven what would otherwise be a mundane set of names and dates. Imagined conversations, decisions and actions have been attached to real people to show how our ancestors lived – and to give my daughter and my grandsons a link into their past.

It has been a long and enthralling journey helped by a global confection of many willing co-researchers, distant kinfolk and archivists.

My previous book, *From Paupers to iPads*, cast the net far and wide, hauling in a diverse catch from those initial fishing trips into my family history. It did, however, produce one overriding and surprising fact: my heritage is Welsh. My direct male line uncoils over four generations to the wildly beautiful, and thankfully mostly unspoilt, westernmost county of Pembrokeshire.

It has much in common – an ancient language, a wild Atlantic coast, a seafaring history – with Cornwall, another Celtic outpost of Britain where I now live. But it was only after settling here that I was hit by the stunning revelation that I have Cornish ancestry too. And to this Celtic melange can be added a few strands of Scottish heritage.

Thus the young man who grew up staunchly believing he was a Man of Kent (that is, born east of the Medway) has late in life found that is but a very minor part of his history. He is a Celt and his roots lie way out west on the magnificent Pembrokeshire coast.

Hence this book and its title which is more focused in its subjects and more selective in its coverage than its predecessor.

TONY BERRY,
Cornwall, 2019

THE FRENCH CONNECTION

THERE WERE NO DEEP thoughts of a Celtic heritage when I first began wondering about my family's past. The idea of trawling through parish records, newspaper archives, censuses and libraries, hoping to discover our roots, simply did not occur. That was something done by academics cloistered in fusty rooms.

I knew all I needed to: everything was centred on Gillingham, the town in Kent where I was born, as was my mother. The immediate family all lived nearby – my mother's parents, Nan from Sussex and Gramp from Yorkshire, and dad's father and stepmother (of whose background I knew very little), plus regular sightings of an assortment of aunts, uncles and cousins visiting from slightly further afield.

They were simply there, a walk-on cast of extras who peopled my existence and needed no explaining.

It never occurred to ask how stocky, bluff, hard-as-nails Gramp, a dyed-in-the-wool York- shireman, got together with Nan, the shy, willowy, almost frail Sussex maid. Both were very much working class, living at the extremes of England in days when the divide between north and south was even greater than it is today and travelling the great distance between them would have been almost unthought of. How and where they met thus remains a mystery never likely to be answered other than by some fictional imaginings.

Nan and Gramp on a wartime visit to our home in Fleetwood c. 1943

It was not until many decades later, when living in Australia, that a faint spark of interest in my ancestry was first dimly lit by a coupling of coincidences. The first occurred while making a working visit to France in my then role as travel editor of Melbourne's highly esteemed daily broadsheet, *The Age*. My route made a brief excursion into an area frequently signposted as the departement (once a dukedom and then a province) of Berry. It was a cause for a passing mix of comment, amusement and conjecture to see the family name so frequently prominent in a foreign land. The second spark to my interest came soon after when I acquired a luxurious book dedicated to *Les Très Riches Heures du Duc de Berry*, a magnificent illustrated manuscript created between 1413 and 1416 by John, the first Duke of Berry and now preserved in the Condé Museum in Chantilly.

Was this ornate and detailed creation the work of my ancestor?

As I slowly turned the pages of John of Berry's awesome manuscript, marvelling at this wondrous creation, I unwittingly took my first steps towards joining the worldwide community of those dreamers and eternal optimists known as family historians.

They sit on their suburban blocks spurred on by the fantasy that the ancestral home is a château in the Loire or a grand mansion nestled in hectares of English woodland. They leap across the centuries imagining notable forebears, members of the landed gentry, royalty, or even the sources of unclaimed fortunes. I was no longer the middle class descendant of lower class strivers, labourers, farm hands, mill workers, workhouse residents and paupers but envisioned myself with roots deep in an ancient region of France that embraces the great chateaux of the Loire Valley and such noble cities as Bourges, Chartres, Tours and Joan of Arc's fateful Orleans.

Flitting through my mind were fanciful visions of a distant and noble patriarch riding forth with banners waving at the head of a troop of loyal supporters and that the Berry family's first steps on to English turf were a result of the Norman invasion. And why not? As I then discovered, the family name lives on in many places only a short boat trip, even a determined swim, across the Channel from my own birthplace in Kent.

Here was my first, admittedly remote, vague and unproven, Celtic connection.

The strongest of Gaul's Celtic tribes, the Bituriges Cubi, occupied Berry around 600 BC. It later became part of the Roman province of Aquitania Prima, was passed to the Franks in the sixth century and then was ruled by a line of hereditary nobles until 1200, when the French kings gained control and in 1360 created the title Duke of Berry.

John, the creator of the illustrated manuscript and third son of King John II, was the first holder of the title. Although said to have been a mediocre and greedy warlord, he was also a notable patron who enjoyed art, music, hunting and good food. He sounded like a man after my own heart; an excellent candidate for ancestor status. He collected precious manuscripts, jewels, enamels, tapestries, birds and exotic animals and sponsored the best artists.

Oh that our heritage could lay claim to an association with this glorious treasure of the Middle Ages – and with the passionate patron who made it possible.

Sadly, John's artistic indulgences severely taxed his estates and he was deeply in debt when he died in Paris in 1416. As there was no surviving male issue the title was recreated for his great-nephew, the Dauphin John, Duke of Touraine, eldest son of King Charles VI, who died shortly afterwards. Various other lesser royals (including two Margarets) were given the title over the following centuries until it came to an abrupt end with Duke Charles Ferdinand's assassination in 1820.

So, after the spendthrift glory days of John – an ordinary moniker that appears often throughout my own family tree – the French clan that bore the Berry name did little of merit and slowly drifted into oblivion.

I have tried to attain glory by association on visits to the bucolic Berry countryside and the glorious Chartres Cathedral. I even stayed a couple of luxuriously memorable nights at Château de Chambord and Château de Chenonceaux where, no doubt, the Berrys once rested and roistered.

Unfortunately, try as I might and willing so hard for it to be true, not one of them can be linked to our much humbler line of Berrys.

This same rampant optimism later led me to explore the magnificent Manorbier Castle – an arrow's flight from my ancestral roots in south Wales. It was built by the du Barri (Berry?) family in Norman times when the spelling of names took numerous variations. This excursion was another false trail but at least it provided the semblance of an ancestral link by way of the castle's network of tunnels used by the smugglers once pursued along the Pembrokeshire coast by my great-great-grandfather.

However, it is good to dream. As family historians soon discover, that is much of what genealogy is about. It is the spur that urges us ancestor-seekers to persevere.

And, as the intervening years have since proved, my Celtic connections not only exist but are far stronger than I ever imagined.

STARTING OUT

As the Kent-born son of a Kentish maid and a Devonian lad, with direct lines back to Sussex and Yorkshire on the maternal side and to Scotland and Wales on the paternal side, the thought never occurred that there might be Cornish blood in my veins. Even with the family's move to the famed Cornish port of Falmouth in the 1950s, there was no suggestion we might have any Kernow connections. We were 'furriners', and that is how it remained well after mum and dad had passed on.

Nothing changed when I first peered some years back into the then sparse foliage of my family tree. Only when I ventured into the rapid sprouting of innumerable branches and twigs, did my Cornish connections start to emerge.

And there they were - a mixed bunch of thieves, adulterers and sheep-stealers, fortunately offset by other more upright citizens such as lighthouse keepers, stone-cutters and farmers who did the right thing by family and community, including enlisting for service in World War I, some never to return.

The discovery of these somewhat dubious ancestors was made even more exciting by finding they all came from my favourite corner of the county - the wild and rugged shipwreck coast of the Lizard peninsular.

The Lizard on a calmer day

In the same way as Cornwall is a part of Britain yet remains staunchly apart from the rest of the country, so is the Lizard attached to Cornwall yet somehow a separate land. Despite its main approach road slicing through the war-ready firepower of the Culdrose airbase and edging the eerie presence of the Goonhilly satellite station, it remains an ancient and mysterious place. A perpetually windswept landscape of forbidding coastal paths, secret coves and closed communities. It is a place of legends and mysteries, of treacherous tides, of shipwrecks accidental and deliberate, and of family feuds and fights.

Fortunately, from a family historian's point of view, the forebears I found are not mere names on a tree. Over time, I have been able to discover the detail of their existence, where and how they lived, and to flesh them out and picture their lives.

There has been much use made of usual sources such as the census and parish records but still more has been unearthed from documents held at the Cornwall Record Office, the ever-growing British Newspaper Archive and from the records of Trinity House.

By delving beyond the 'hints' thrown up online by such genealogical stalwarts as Ancestry and Find My Past and seeking innumerable alternative sources, our ancestors can be restored to life; making them living people rather than mere names listed on a GEDCOM, the name given to electronic files basic to the sharing of information among genealogists.

Despite their status as 'furriners' and 'emmets', as the parochial and patriotic true Cornish love to label the incomers, my family remained in Falmouth. Eventually they were accepted and became acknowledged minor pillars of the local community. My sister, Judy, married a dyed-in-the-wool Cornishman. And their two daughters, my nieces of Cornish birth, have since added to the male and female side. Thus, although I am the last to bear the name along this Berry line, the family tree now not only has roots in Wales but also in this other Celtic land.

My final years of education were spent here, followed by my indentured first steps into a lifelong career as journalist, editor and author. While the family remained in Cornwall, I moved away in pursuit of a profession that eventually took me to live on the other side of world. Fortunately, a long period as a travel writer enabled me to make frequent return trips and, though always as a tourist, there gradually developed a deep feeling of being at one with this magical land and that this was a place where I 'belonged'.

Memories remain vivid of accompanying dad as he drove out to remote clifftops and darkened fishing villages. These random visits were to check that men of HM Customs who patrolled the coast were keeping to their schedules. Their rosters changed weekly so that smugglers could never be sure when a patrolman would appear, binoculars scanning the sea for illegal imports.

What lad brought up on a reading list of *Masterman Ready, Mr Midshipman Easy* and *The Boys Own Paper* could not be enthralled by these mini adventures, often on the darkest and wildest of nights?

Added to these captivating moments were the three years spent between school and national service as an apprentice journalist (fully indentured in the old style) with the august, historic and once highly respected *West Briton*. That was in an era when newspapers still faithfully documented the minutiae of community life and reporters relied not on phone calls and press releases but spent their time mingling with their readers. It was also when words, phrasing and punctuation were meticulously checked and corrected with stern reminders to avoid committing any further crimes against the English language.

One of my weekly tasks was to tour through all the hamlets and villages of the Lizard Peninsula, gathering snippets of all manner of news from a very mixed bag of correspondents in shops, churches, manses, pubs and private homes. The 'news' was of church gatherings, parish meetings, fetes, garden shows, jumble sales, school sports, hunt meets and the inevitable births, marriages, and obituaries.

Hardly a hillock, hamlet or harbour escaped my attention. I saw this still wild land in all seasons, all that the weather gods could throw up out of the Atlantic or blow in across Goonhilly Downs, where the giant dishes of the tracking station are about to gain a new life as an essential link in international space communications. It was also the period when the murderous myxomatosis ran rife through the rabbit population. This extreme control measure resulted in a painful and lingering death, with dazed and dying rabbits becoming a hazard that drivers were unable to avoid.

Little did I know that in making this weekly journey through Mullion, Landewednack, Kynance, Coverack, Cury, Cadgwith and Ruan Minor I was following in the footsteps of my ancestors. People with names such as Jose, Gilbert, Tripp and Morrish. Names found in church-yards throughout the peninsula and engraved, too, on the area's war memorials in lasting tribute to those who went away and never returned.

Wolf Rock lighthouse where Charles Nicholas was working as a keeper when he met Sidonia.

Some of them, admittedly, are fairly remote ancestrally, mere twiglets on the outer branches of the family tree. But others are close enough to be considered 'family' and well entitled to be warmly invited to any imagined gathering of the clan.

Certainly, none more so than first cousin Charles Edwin Nich-olas. He not only married into one of the Lizard's most deeply entrenched Cornish families but was also the son of my great-grand-aunt Agness Berry of Milford Haven, that Welsh port from where all my Berry ancestors emerged.

It was while serving as a lighthouse-keeper at the famed Lizard Light and earlier at Wolf Rock, way out in the Atlantic between Land's End and the Scilly Isles, that Charles somehow found time and opportunity to court and marry a Cornish girl with the wonderful name, among others, of Sidonia who came from a long-established family of Lizard area serpentine miners and stone carvers.

It was therefore thanks to Charles that the Berry family's link between the two Celtic nations was firmly forged.

But, as they say in those irritating TV adverts, there was more. Agness was the daughter of John Berry, the tidewaiter and Customs officer who was the great-grandfather of my own Customs officer father, Wilfred Berkeley Berry, whose own father had been born in Scotland of Welsh parents.

Thus, the Celtic link about which my parents never knew, along with the Customs officer connection, was stronger than anyone could ever have imagined.

So, back to the beginning, or at least to the middle distance, which is as far as reliable records so far discovered make possible ....

EMAILS CAN BE RELATIVE

EMAILS ARE DISTURBINGLY INSTANT, not only in the way they drop unannounced into a computer's Inbox but also in the way they confront the recipient. There is no puzzling over the sender's identity as there is with an unexpected letter received by snail mail. There is no examining the postmark, no pondering the handwriting, wondering about the sender and the contents. It is on your desktop and in your face.

Thus did a hitherto unknown cousin called Lynne reveal her existence. It set in train a journey both of us had only vaguely considered and which I thought I was destined to travel alone. Both had been tracing our family histories – she in Cornwall, in England's wild southwest, and me in the inner suburbs of Melbourne, the cosmopolitan state capital of Victoria and Australia's heartland of culture and caffeine.

Her probing, much deeper and far more efficient than mine, had taken her back to the 1840s when one of her line had hitched up with one of my line. The knots were tied and, three generations later, we were entwined as cousins.

Lynne's was not the only contact received via cyberspace. Once I began making my sapling of a family tree visible online, other previously unheard-of relatives emerged in Bournemouth, Essex, Swindon, Wales, Cornwall, California and Yorkshire, and then in the wider world.

But Lynne was by far the most persistent and positive. A shared enthusiasm for ancestral detection was evident very early on. Even better, her emails were literate and witty. They showed a quirky sense of humour based on a love of words and language. The rapport was as instant as hot water and Nescafe, and much more to my liking than that dubious brew.

The exchange of information became more frequent, confirming the relationship and throwing up even more links. Lynne's home was less than a kilometre from that of my sister and at one stage they had lived only a few houses apart totally unaware of their ancestral ties. Stranger still, it emerged that in much earlier times our two families had lived in similar close proximity as neighbours and workmates in Pembrokeshire in the southwest corner of Wales.

Within weeks email contact was dispensed with in favour of instantaneous exchanges through the wonder of Skype by voice and video. Genealogy had never been so much fun, nor so instantaneous. Thanks to the internet, research that only a few years ago would have been a lengthy and painstaking task now took only moments. Data could be exchanged, debated and analysed at the press of a button.

Gradually a vague thought of someday walking the streets of my fore-bears blossomed into an undeniable urge. With every new detail uncovered and as each personal trait was revealed there was an exciting inevitability about our relationship. And so began an intensely personal odyssey that took me way beyond the mere compilation of a mundane family tree with its clusters of boxes linking names across the generations. Family research took on a whole new meaning and among my kith and kin the phrase became a euphemism for something other than delving into dusty archives.

My journey took me from Melbourne via London to Lynne's home in the Cornish cathedral city of Truro and, together, on to the hilly streets of ancient Haverfordwest in the far southwest corner of Wales. There, within the solid walls of the ruined castle that looms over the town, we pored over parish records, archives, manuscripts and maps helped by a friendly staff with a seemingly inexhaustible knowledge of the region's past.

We soon learned family researchers need to be precise in their enquiries and to go armed with definite questions. To enter any records office and state you are researching the Smith family will get you nowhere in a long time. Success is far more likely by saying, for example, that you are trying to trace the marriage of John Smith from such and such a parish around 1815. Old handwritten documents will be speedily produced and you will be directed where next to look in your research.

Our two mornings in Haverfordwest Castle produced marriage records, two wills made in the 1780s, details of family donations to a village school, an invaluable map and the revelation of a coroner's report into a family member's death of which we had no previous knowledge.

This latter document provided evidence that the family had lived at an address in Pembroke Dock some thirty years earlier than we had previously thought. We were off and running like foxhounds finding a new scent. There were streets to walk, houses to find and mysteries to solve.

Chief among the latter was the whereabouts of the village of Coombs where censuses showed my great-great-great-grandparents once lived. There is no doubt Coombs existed way back in the medieval era, but at some time over the past hundred years or so it seems to have been wiped off the map. It definitely existed in 1851 when John Berry, his wife Ann (nee Hughes) and their ten children were recorded in the census as living 'in the last house in the village of Coombs'.

Milford Haven modern marina sits alongside the original Custom House where John Berry was a tidewaiter

It was a community within the parish of Steynton, a strip of land six miles from north to south and no more than two miles from east to west. In the 1830s Steynton was recorded as having a population of 3000. Many of these, however, would have lived in the borough of Milford, the seaport and market town on the shores of Milford Haven, which formed the parish's southern boundary.

At high tide, a tidal inlet, the Hubbertson Pill, provided small craft with access to Coombs from the broad harbour beyond, and from there to the wild open sea. Although largely agricultural, the parish also contained deposits of culm that were extracted at a mine on Lord Kensington's nearby estate and provided the district with cheap fuel.

Extensive searches proved the village once existed along the creeks flowing inland from the vast waterway that is now Milford harbour. However, a painstaking trawl through the archives eventually dashed all hopes of retracing my forebears' footsteps. Coombs was still there in 1880, according to a map of Pembrokeshire produced by the archivists beavering away in the castle's Public Record Office. But not even their willing determination could produce any references more recent than that. It had vanished, gone without a trace. Neither the intensely detailed Ordnance Survey maps nor the usually reliable Google maps recognised its existence.

We were two days into a tour of the area when we had one of those Eureka moments beloved by family historians. In a tourist guide to Milford Haven, picked up as we rifled through a rack of brochures in the hotel foyer, was that elusive name: Coombs – surely its only inclusion on a modern map. It was precisely where I believed it should have been. It was simply a word in an otherwise blank space as if the artist felt the need to put something there.

All roads may very well lead to Rome, but still we found none that led to Coombs. As testimony to the past there was, however, the Coombs Road turning off the main route from the medieval community of Steynton (where my folks later lived) to the modern port of Milford Haven that later subsumed it.

Little more than a country lane, Coombs Road plunges and twists its way down to the muddy and tidal Pill Creek before hair-pinning up the other side to Venn Farm and Castle Hall, which were both prominent on maps of John Berry's time. A minor industrial estate now stands where a vineyard once struggled for existence in a climate hardly conducive to viticulture. A quarry and lime kilns are now also nothing more than landmarks on old maps.

On the track to Coombs

A few clicks of the milometer past Venn Farm we noticed one of those ubiquitous walking man signs indicating a footpath heading off to the left in the direction of the woods and Pill Creek. To this pair of seekers of the past, this was no ordinary indicator. It was a true sign in the fullest, almost biblical, sense; surely a pointer to our holy grail.

We followed the rough narrow trail between fenced-off farm meadows, slowly descending towards the thickly wooded slopes bordering the creek. On either side were the remnants of thick old stone walls barely discernable beneath masses of brambles and undergrowth. Someone had once lived here.

The final few metres sloped steeply down then broadened out to a gravelly creek bed. A lively stream flowed out of dense woods on our right, rippling over a ford and on into the creek. The view to our left opened out, the creek widening into a broad expanse of mudflats and minor streams rimmed by wooded hillsides.

I was home!

This was where my direct ancestors lived; the wellspring and source of the many Berrys that followed. Somewhere up to the right, among the tree-covered slopes and overlooking the bend in the creek, was as far back as I had been able to trace my existence.

A light breeze ruffled the branches. A weak September sun dappled the water. It was such a peaceful and almost hidden corner of this troubled and angry world.

I stood there in numbed silence, close to tears. This was not the time for words.

The emotion-fuelled walk back to Coombs Road set me on the next stage of a journey that has transpired as a long and winding trail eventually resulting in the pages that follow and much more that has yet to be told.

Only some years later did I make the connection between the vanished community of Coombs, my own father and those other Celtic kinfolk on the wild shores of Cornwall. And it all began, so far as this story is concerned, with great-great-grandfather John Berry.

Before him there was his father, Joseph, a cabinetmaker like so many of my ancestors. Of his father, another John, little is known other than he was born in Pembrokeshire and married Sarah Robling at Roch on 20 October 1770 – my 4x great-grandparents.

CROSSING BRIDGES

The magnificent Severn Bridge, one of two crossings from England into Wales

THERE IS A SYMBOLIC synchronicity about taking the main road routes into my two ancestral 'homelands'. Whether going to Wales or Cornwall, there is a spectacular bridge to cross. Each is perched high above a river that provides an unavoidable and very clearly defined boundary.

Travellers are left in no doubt that they are crossing a significant border; a sharp contrast that has far more impact than the usual mundane and imaginary bureaucratic point in a road indicated by the obligatory county council signpost.

The greeting on the Severn Bridge

These are national boundaries (yes, Cornwall considers itself a country), even if there are no Customs posts, visa checks or vehicle searches. England is being left behind. On the far side of these impressive engineering achievements, lie foreign lands – Cymru on the other side of the rivers

Severn and Wye, and Kernow on the opposite banks of the Tamar. Both use their traditional languages on their signposts of welcome.

Even now, many years on from my first crossing of Brunel's imposing span across the Tamar, there is a frisson of excitement, tangled emotions and sense of arrival each time I see the sign, *Kernow a'gas dynergh*. A homecoming for the prodigal in so many ways.

But nothing in my genealogical journeys quite prepared me for the sensation felt at the end of the high-rise 1.6 kilometre crossing of the two rivers that for centuries helped the Welsh repel invaders from England and beyond.

It was tempting to seek comparisons with facing East German police on my way through Checkpoint Charlie or arriving in China when it was still forbidden territory behind the Bamboo Curtain; perhaps even gunpoint confrontations in Amman on my way through Jordan to Israel. All big border moments in my earlier life.

But they came with stress, anxiety, even fear of what lay beyond; the sense of passing the point of no return. Not so on this border with its big *Croeso i Gymru* sign (which is a language lesson in itself) assuring a welcome nowadays awaits all incomers … even the English.

Plenty of emotions rapidly surfaced, rippling through my body, unbidden and unexpected. They were, however, underscored by excitement, by thoughts of discovery; a child's Christmas morning impatience and wonder at what unwrapping the parcels beneath the tree would reveal.

The excitement and expectations grew as we trundled on westwards, the traffic greatly diminishing once we had bypassed the major cities of Swansea and Cardiff and their industrial neighbours. Smaller towns, more villages, spreading open countryside, a distant backdrop of hills and mountains on our right, glimpses of coastline and sea to our left.

Eventually, after more miles than we had imagined, we were winding through the narrow hilly streets of historic Pembroke, its ancient riverside castle still standing as a fearsome fortress and reminder of the war-torn centuries of the past.

There has been a castle on this site since 1083. Initially it was a fort built of earth and wood. Richard I gifted it to William Marshal in 1189 and he transformed it into the imposing and solid stone castle that remains today. In a cosy pub less than an arrow's flight from its dominating ramparts, doubtless filled with nerves and trepidation similar to our own, living proof of my Welsh ancestry awaited.

Recognition was instant. Cousin Amanda's broad smile was spontaneous and welcoming, followed immediately by a warm embrace. All nerves vanished.

Lunch was ordered, conversation flowed the way it does between close friends. Questions of who, when and where peppered our lengthy chat in scenes reminiscent of the long-running television tear-jerker *Long Lost Family*. And no scripts or prompts were needed.

At moments such as these, family history is transformed from a mostly solo and impersonal pastime of data collection into something wonderfully personal and meaningful. A family tree on paper or computer suddenly blossoms into life. Real flesh and blood people emerge from the dense foliage of names, dates and places. All those hours spent scouring the census, searching through church records, sourcing birth marriage and death certificates and generally verifying facts suddenly become worthwhile.

Since that memorable meeting of the three cousins – myself, Lynne and Amanda – we have kept in close touch, as kinfolk rather than as researchers and yet also extending our shared knowledge of our Berry family. Through Amanda I have discovered more cousins and other family deeply entrenched further along the coast in Swansea, many with that constant thread of maritime connections. And from there I discovered an extension, also created by that seafaring trait, now rooted in the US West Coast but which a hundred years earlier suffered a seafaring tragedy on British shores.

That initial journey into Wales and our happy meeting in a Pembroke pub was far more significant than I ever envisaged it could be. It roused feelings that had lain dormant for years; feelings that I was only vaguely aware existed and which at first were hard to explain or define. There have been so many unexpected emotional moments in the succeeding years, most of them unheralded and arriving with all the surprise of a mugger's punch in the ribs.

Only now, some years on and several visits later, do I realise it is a strong sense of belonging. It matters little whether I am making the journey across the Tamar into Cornwall or over that spectacular span high above the Severn and the Wye to Wales, or even doing these trips in reverse. Either way, an inner voice sings out; a reminder that I am a Celt crossing bridges, in so many senses of that phrase, as he moves between his two ancient homes.

After almost eight decades I have gained a genuine sense of identity. I now know where I truly belong.

The original and continuing mainspring for my ongoing discoveries in Wales has been my lunchtime 'date' in that Pembroke pub, the fittingly red-haired Welsh maid Amanda. Her emergence as a cousin played a major role in so much that has been unearthed since.

From that first face-to-face meeting, the willing and friendly exchange of information has seen our trees flourish from mere saplings to sturdy growths, thrusting out their branches far and wide.

Our connections stem from three generations ago with the marriage in Swansea on 11 May 1893 of dressmaker Florence Rosena Berry, daughter of John Berry, son of my great-great-grandfather, another John Berry, to much-travelled mariner Frederick William Richardson.

One of their sons, also named Frederick William Richardson, married Winifred Brice and fathered Florence B Richardson. Florence wed William Frank Jones on a winter's day in Haverfordwest in January 1953 and together they became the parents of Amanda, my 'date' for lunch in a Pembroke pub more than a hundred years after the links between our families were first forged.

This connection to the Brice family did give our otherwise staunchly Celtic line a small injection of Devonian blood by virtue of Winifred's father, William, being born in Devon. However, any Devonian influence on our family trees was soon diminished and he moved to the Welsh industrial town of Neath some time in his late teens and found work as a copper smelter. There he married Welsh girl Mary Ann Lloyd and over the years become father to four sons and five daughters, all eventually creating more branches on our Celtic tree, including the one that produced cousin Amanda, her parents Florence and William, and her three siblings.

Others led to Berry-linked enclaves in Swansea and on the US West Coast in California, all of which are still thriving, and to the one to which I have now returned in Cornwall.

Amanda's own line has taken detours into the Southend area of Essex, going from the farthest side of the country in the west to its most easterly on the shores of the English Channel.

But she and her roots still remain deeply fixed in wild and rugged west Wales with ancestral connections to its land and rural industries. For some kinfolk, a background in foundry work and blacksmithing ensured a natural progression from servicing the area's horse-drawn transport into meeting the demands of the dawning era of the motor car.

Notable among these was Amanda's grandfather, John Henry Jones, who started out as an apprentice blacksmith at the dawn of the twentieth century and progressed to being the owner of J.H. Jones Victoria Garage in Milford Haven. This substantial business not only provided repair and maintenance services to car owners but also, in those days long before the likes of Hertz, Avis and Europcar, hired out vehicles.

The Jones family garage in Milford Haven
[picture courtesy of cousin Amanda Jones]

As for the rest of the many cousins, uncles, nephews and nieces who spread this flourishing offshoot of my Celtic tree, that is up to Amanda to reveal such as she knows and is willing to relate.

That is her story to tell while I proceed with my own Celtic tale …

A SENSE OF BELONGING

I FIRST ARRIVED IN Cornwall several decades ago as a total stranger. I knew nothing and cared even less about this wild and ancient land. Uppermost in my mind as an introverted teenager was how to cope with induction into yet another school, the ninth, where loyalties would be long set and any newcomer faced an inevitable uphill battle for acceptance.

This situation was made all the worse by having to pass scrutiny and make connections a mere six weeks before the end of the school year. Then came the long summer holiday break. And, eight weeks later, I had to start all over again.

Always spruce and tidy – my father Wilfred B Berry reporting for HM Customs duty in Greenock on the Clyde in 1945

My reluctant arrival in this most south-westerly and often bleak corner of the country, where the locals referred to newcomers as 'furriners' and 'emmets', was the result of my father's posting as chief preventive officer to the HM Customs and Excise headquarters in Falmouth.

This later turned out to be the final move in a nomadic existence around Britain's ports and harbours that had kept our family on the move for the past sixteen years.

There was no place I could truly call home; we belonged nowhere. My life had been a succession of dwellings, none of them sufficiently distinctive nor lived in long enough to leave an impression worth recalling in later years.

Likewise with the several schools I had attended, or rather passed through. These had produced steadily diminishing returns in academic achievement and even less in lasting friendships.

Even a trainee psychiatrist would have little trouble in ascribing to these early years my gradual development into an introverted, self-sufficient, and somewhat anti-social loner. Yet one who has always been content with his aloneness. As Sartre contended, *Hell is other people*. And so it is how my life has been shaped and thus, in some minds, qualified me for lifelong honorary membership of *Grumpy Old Men*, although I would contend outward appearances can often be deceptive.

The move to Cornwall meant our few closest relatives were close to three hundred arduous miles away. These were pre-motorway days of low-powered cars and pollution-created fogs, or smogs, as they were frequently called in acknowledgement of the coal-fired smoke that was often their root cause. There were no such things as a 'short break to visit Nan' or a 'quick trip to town' (meaning London). Every journey was a major expedition of intricate planning, packed meals, snail's pace progress and total exhaustion for all involved. Something to avoid at all costs.

We were isolated, marooned, and friendless. Robinson Crusoes in our own land. Or, rather, in a land where many still believed England came to an abrupt end at the River Tamar and Cornwall, the ancient kingdom of King Arthur, bardic rites and moorland mysteries began.

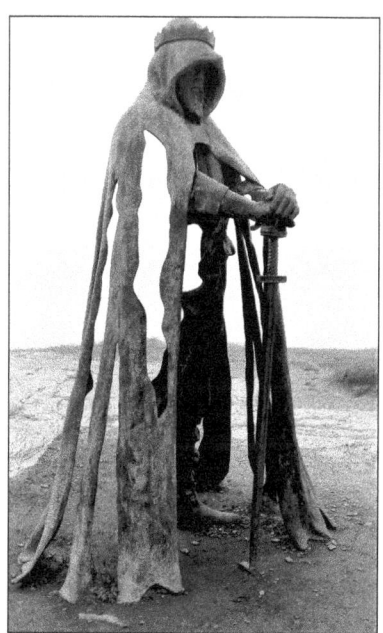

Ever mystic and mysterious Cornwall – guarded by King Arthur atop the cliffs at Tintagel

If only I had known then at least something of what I have since discovered as the result of this late-life decision to research my family's past. Sadly, it is only through this recent exploration that an exciting aspect to our relocation has emerged; one that inevitably arouses almost daily thoughts of the 'what if?' variety.

Would what I have since unearthed have wrought changes in our attitudes and in ourselves?

How would my discoveries have affected our relationships to our new surroundings and our slow acceptance by those who saw us as 'furriners'?

The decision by his lords and masters at HM Board of Customs and Excise to install my father as boss cocky in Falmouth meant the entire Cornish coastline was now his fiefdom. This gave him extraordinary powers over some six hundred miles of frequently storm-swept coves, headlands, beaches and treacherous inlets where, for centuries, the inhabitants had regarded smuggling as a way of life which, if not actually engaged in, was at least to be supported.

What dad never knew was that he was following in the footsteps of his great-grandfather who, a hundred years earlier, toiled as a tidewaiter - the forerunner of the modern Customs officer - on the waters of the Welsh port of Milford Haven.

From this ancestor, there descended a veritable tribe of mariner types who, like dad, never strayed far from coastal habitats. As the trail unravelled down the years, its branches soon wound their way into Cornwall to establish links with those whose roots already lay deep in its ancient soil. These were our Cousin Jacks, as the Cornish have long been known wherever in the world they have settled.

My discoveries came only gradually to light. As explained earlier, they occurred as the result of a whim sparked by late-life research into my family tree that spurred me into leaving Australia in 2010 and moving back to Cornwall's cathedral city of Truro. From there, subsequent explorations led to the discovery that not only were the family's origins to be found along the beautiful and magical Welsh coastline of Pembrokeshire and on the banks of the Clyde in Scotland but also that we really did belong on this side of the Tamar.

Whichever way you look at it, we are far more Celtic than English.

All those early years spent wandering around Britain and, for a large chunk of my life, living in Australia, had been the journey of a soul lost in the wilderness; an endless searching for identity and that all-important sense of belonging.

In the closing stages of his life, this prodigal son had at last come home.

I belonged.

And now it was time to go back to my roots before too much more time was wasted.

A COTTAGE BY THE CREEK

IT WAS A TERRIBLE January day in 1849 in the worker's cottage at the furthest end of the Welsh village of Coombs. It was the very depth of winter, numbingly cold and endlessly wet. Such roads as existed were mostly little more than rutted, muddy tracks that had long turned into quagmires. The packed mud floors of the cottage were scarcely much better. There were no floorboards. The chilling damp percolated into every corner. Rain seeped through the straw roof into the two rooms that housed John Berry, his wife and eight children, four of them born in the past nine years.

Now another was on its way, without benefit of heating, running water or indoor sanitation. For Ann Berry, much as she was used to regular confinements, this must have been one of the worst. Why else would the churchgoing Ann tell husband John, tidewaiter and Customs officer, that they would name the new arrival Jabez? She knew the name carried only one meaning: born in pain.

Its source was the line in Chronicles 4:9-10: *His mother called his name Jabez, saying 'because I bore him with sorrow'.* Chronicles also says Jabez is '*a well-respected man and an ancestor in the lineage of the king's tribe of Judah whose prayer to God for blessing was answered.*' There was a brief period in the eighteenth and nineteenth centuries when the name's biblical connotations overruled its more negative side. However, it soon fell into disrepute and nowadays does not even figure on the list of the one thousand most popular names.

My great-great-grandfather, who gave his mother such a hard time in emerging from her womb on January 31, 1849, thus became one of the few children who have been burdened with the name of Jabez. Fortunately for him, his parents also preceded it with an Alfred. This was the only time a Jabez label appeared in the Berry family. But the Alfred tag lived on for two more generations.

Fourteen-year-old Agness, the couple's oldest daughter, had made the trek from Milford, where she was living with her grandparents while working as an apprentice dressmaker. She was well-used to the groans and writhings of giving birth and hardly heeded the stern orders of a village midwife, who had little patience with women who made a fuss about nature's routine.

As Agness proudly showed her mother the newly-delivered Alfred Jabez, the rest of her siblings gathered around - two-year-old William, four-year-old Emma, seven-year-old Elizabeth, eight-year-old Joseph, eleven-year-old Edwin. and twelve-year-old John. All squashed together for there was nowhere else for this brood to go other than outdoors in the cold and mire.

Standard living in my ancestors' times – typical thatched Welsh cottage

Only eighteen-year-old Douglas escaped hearing his mother's agonising cries. He was absent plying his trade as an apprentice shipwright in the Pembroke dockyard. It was more than his job and his future were worth to miss a day working for a master to whom he was rigorously bound for the next three years.

This was communal living at its most cramped. A report to one of several nineteenth century royal commissions described the ordinary cottage in south Wales at the time as: *'a rectangular building about 20 feet by 12 (inside measurement) with walls of mud (clay and straw mixed) or stone about 8 feet high'.*

Thus John, Ann and their brood lived in a space about the size of the average display home lounge room. Privacy was an unknown pleasure for, as the royal commission noted, *'Running back from each side of the door for 6 or 8 feet, and almost as high as the door are partitions, often formed by the back of a box bed or chest of drawers, by means of which partitions the inside space is divided into two small rooms, in one of which is a wide fireplace surmounted by a conical chimney.'*

Another account, written in 1814, described these squalid cottages as having, *'a mud walling of about 5 feet high, a hipped end, low roofing of straw with a wattle and daub chimney, kept together with hay rope bandages, and frequently from its inclined posture making a very obtuse angle with the gable end over which it hangs'.*

Despite the heartbreaking squalor of these cottages, where there was *'no ventilation except what enters through the doorway and passed out through the chimney'.*

Yet despite the cramped space, basic construction and lack of light and air, the women of the Welsh countryside such as Ann were deemed so conscientious that the commissioner added that, *'except in the north of England and in Scotland, I never saw such a general endeavour to make a poor building look its best'.* And this was despite many women working in the fields throughout the day.

There was little protection from winter's incessant rain – *'The mud cottage is almost always covered with straw thatch'* – and almost no natural light to dispel the gloom – *'In the middle of the front wall is the door with a small window on each side'.*

A Reverend William Owen told the commissioners, *'The whole interior is open to the roof, except where boards or wattled hurdles are stuck across the heads of the walls to support children's beds. The floor is usually of mud or puddled clay. The only outside office is the pigsty, generally built against the end of the cottage. Such is a description of probably four-fifths of the labourers' cottages in the districts I visited'.*

And this was in 1867, almost twenty years after the day teenager Agness Berry helped at the birth of Alfred Jabez, indicating little progress was made in improving the lot of the labouring classes. By then, however, the Berry family – with yet another addition, George in 1851 – had managed to considerably improve their lot.

They had transported their meagre goods and chattels little more than a mile down the road from the hamlet of Coombs – where they were registered in the 1851 census as living at 'the last house'– to the medieval parish of Steynton and then into slightly more substantial premises at 71 Robert Street in the rapidly growing port area taking on an identity of its own under the name of Milford Haven.

WATCHERS BY MOONLIGHT

IT WAS A CRISP wintery night. The headlands and inlets around the wide expanse of Milford Haven's harbour were clearly etched by a moon occasionally hidden by a light veil of scudding clouds. A cluster of seagoing boats rocked gently at anchor in the mainstream, safe from the huge swells of the nearby Atlantic Ocean. Others were safely moored to piers and jetties.

Suddenly, there was a fresh rippling of the water close to the shoreline. Something had disturbed the calm surface. Keen ears could hear the faint sound of oars squeaking in their rowlocks. A skiff rowed by two men emerged from the shadows. The men leaned back and gave a final thrust of their oars to push their craft up on to the pebbled beach.

As they stepped warily on to shore, heaving a bundled load between them, there were shouts from further along. Lanterns threw a flickering light on the scene as two other men emerged from hiding behind a low brick wall. There was confusion, a confrontation. The flash and explosive crack of the powder from a gun being fired shattered the quiet. The boatmen sprinted off. The men with lanterns attempted a half-hearted chase but soon gave up and returned to inspect the bundled package. They took a furtive look around. After a whispered discussion, they hauled the abandoned cargo up the beach and into the shadows.

A cloud drifted across the moon. All was dark and quiet once more.

The following morning, John Berry, my great-great-grandfather, sat with wife Ann at the kitchen table in their cramped two-roomed cottage at the end of a row of similar dwellings clustered alongside a creek a couple of kilometres inland from the harbour. He told her about the incident on the beach the night before.

'They were too quick for us,' he said.

His wife gave a dismissive sniff and wiped a cloth over the rough wooden table.

'Just as well, I'd say. I don't want you coming home cut to pieces by some ne'er do well. Don't know why you ever took that job on. You wouldn't be the first to come home covered in blood or worse.'

John felt it best not to answer. His decision to throw in his job as a joiner and join the Customs service was a running sore between them. It had seemed like a good idea at the time when he weighed up the apparent security of a government job against the haphazard shifts available in the fledgling dockyard. Ann, however, was deeply concerned about the dangers of his new career. And there was another far more disturbing factor: she would rather her husband came home bone-tired and weary from a long shift in the shipyard than have people in the village turn away when she approached.

A tidewaiter ranked low on the social acceptance scale and this flowed through to his wife and family. Most folk saw little harm in the smugglers' activities; many regarded them as benefactors who made essentials such as salt and tallow readily available for a third of the price demanded by storekeepers.

'You'll never win,' said Ann. 'Almost everyone's against you.'

Again, he knew she was right. There were too many stories told in the hotels and on the wharves of otherwise upright citizens who thought nothing of siding with the smugglers rather than supporting the government's law enforcers.

Solva in the 1830s, painting by Henry G Gastineau (image in National Library of Wales)

'Look at that Mr Raymond,' chided Ann. 'Supposed to be so law-abiding.'

John knew the story well. Justice Raymond meted out penalties on local lawbreakers twenty-five kilometres away around the coast at Solva, a narrow inlet on the shores of St Bride's Bay. When a villager decided to chalk up a few brownie points by informing him of the imminent arrival of a cargo of contraband salt, the justice put on a wonderful show of storming down to the harbour. He bellowed his anger as he went, his voice guaranteed loud enough to warn everyone in the area.

By the time he had been ferried out to the allegedly offending vessel there was not a skerrick of salt to be found on board. However, it was strongly rumoured that the waters of Solva Harbour were somewhat saltier than usual in following days. And no one was hauled before Justice Raymond to face charges of smuggling.

John allowed himself a flicker of a smile at the thought.

'It's not funny,' reprimanded Ann, now in full flight on her favourite hobby horse. 'No one was hurt that time. But look what happened over at Pen-y-Bont. I don't want you coming home on a stretcher.' She paused. 'Or worse.'

John knew she had a point and was aware of the incident even though it had occurred more than a day's walk from his own territory. It was one of the worst of many cases in which the smugglers had shown scant regard for the armed force of the law. A notorious local smuggler by the name of Jolly had been leading a team of drovers moving contraband from the shores of Cardigan Bay through to England when they were confronted by the revenue men at Pen-y-Bont. What was described as 'a bloody battle' ensued with dead and dying bodies left behind as the smugglers fled into the hills.

Smuggling heaven – the Pembrokeshire coast

In similar incidents it was often the Customs men who, although armed, came off second best. Only a few years before John Berry joined the service the Pembroke community was shocked and divided by the violence that ended the 'reign' of 'the king of the smugglers', a charismatic local character named William Truscott. This well-known organiser of smuggling rings throughout south Wales was eventually captured at New Quay in one of the caves along Cardigan Bay used for storing smuggled goods. He managed to escape (or was there connivance at his release?) and fled all the way to Pembroke, some eighty kilometres away.

Customs men caught up with him as he was trying to cross the Pembroke River and opened fire. Truscott was hit and wounded. The Customs men claimed the smuggler drowned before anyone could reach him but bystanders alleged the officers ignored his cries for help. An inquest jury agreed and found the revenue officers' action was 'highly reprehensible, cowardly and cruel'. They were never going to win. The entire Pembrokeshire coastline had a long history as a favoured haunt of smugglers, who tended to be more supported than condemned by all levels of society.

John Berry's job title of tidewaiter (or wayter) no longer exists although it aptly defined his daily duty. He was a Customs officer who *waited* for the high tide to bring in the ships. More importantly, he *waited* for the smugglers who were making use of these ships, either as crew or by ferrying in goods to their coastal hideouts. He had to *wait* on board until the ship's cargo was unloaded. A tidewaiter's commissioned duty was to board incoming vessels and check that they dropped anchor at the appointed place in the harbour, making sure the cargo was not unloaded on an isolated jetty out of sight of more senior Customs men known as controllers, and collectors (all no doubt eyeing each other suspiciously). The tidewaiter, too, was under observation – from a tide surveyor.

According to *The Letter-Book of John Byrd, Customs Collector of South East Wales 1648-80* (edited by S.K. Roberts) a tidewaiter was a job low on the rungs of the civil service ladder. Great-great-grandfather John would nonetheless have needed to be sufficiently literate and numerate to pass the Civil Service examination for tidewaiters. It was a test which would have stretched the abilities of many of today's students, who are so deeply dependent upon their iPads, pocket calculators and spellcheckers.

John not only had to prove he could write, but also that he could do so clearly, with correct spelling and an understanding of a word's current usage. The examination also posed several questions to test his arithmetic.

A Guide to the Civil Service Examinations, compiled by P S King in 1856, asked would-be tidewaiters to divide 59,436,784,379 by 492 and wanted to know how many square inches there were in 50 acres. Or how about calculating the number of loads of hewn timber in 2,160,000 cubic inches? Those taking the exam had to add columns of money, weights, volume and length. Tests of subtraction, multiplication (978,015,632 by 9,738) and division (95,708,654 by 298) completed their ordeal, although it is difficult to visualise when such complex and extended calculations would be required.

In John Berry's time, the effectiveness of the country's war on smuggling varied greatly according to the calibre of the officers, their pay and conditions, and other factors. When pay was good, and the service was able to hire committed and diligent officers who could call on the military for assistance, the preventive effort could be remarkably effective.

Sadly, this happy state seemed to exist for only a minority of the time. The riding officers who patrolled much of the coast were not only poorly paid but also had to dip into their £42 annual salary to buy and maintain their horses. Little wonder that even a small denomination banknote was enough to see a blind eye turned when a contraband run was on.

Corruption and disloyalty were not limited to the lawmakers and there was little joy for those who tried to do the right thing. Ann Berry remembered as a child hearing the story doing the rounds of a woman who found her husband had stowed a cargo of smuggled French brandy in the cellar of their Swanlake home.

The woman decided to make a quick (and secret) two hundred pounds for herself by informing the Customs officers and collecting a reward. Unfortunately, she couldn't resist telling her plan to a friend who then told the woman's husband. The smuggler quickly rounded up his mates and the barrels of booze were well on their way to happy buyers when the Customs men arrived to face an empty cellar.

The scene of this incident was within walking distance of the magnificent spread of Manorbier Castle, a slightly off-the-beaten track treasure harking back to Norman times which was at the centre of the nineteenth century smuggling trade. It was here that a larger than life character named Captain Jack Furze conned the locals into letting him take over the lease of the farm attached to the castle.

He spun a yarn about having saved some money from his seafaring days and that he would now devote his energies to running the farm and digging for coal while still doing a bit of coastal trading in his brig, the *Jane*. The locals soon discovered the coastal trading was more to do with illicit barrels of brandy than anything else and the digging was to create tunnels for escape and storage rather than prospect for coal.

Manorbier Castle remained a hotbed of smuggling activity until Jolly Jack's little boat was fired on and almost run down by a Royal Navy ship. The cruiser crushed the decking of the *Jane* and pursued it relent- lessly until nightfall forced it to call off the chase. The incident convinced Captain Furze he had had enough of danger and he opted for a quieter life. Two cen- turies later, the smugglers' tunnels still honeycomb the ground beneath Manorbier Castle as testimony to the extent of the captain's thriving illegal trade.

On the contraband trail – the author at Manobier Castle

Hearing that the navy had crushed Jolly Jack's boat and set the man on a more legal path did little to comfort Ann Berry. Such victories were few for the law enforcers and the danger they faced was too great. Smugglers had been known to ram the Customs patrol boats, even to board them and attack the officers, forcing them to flee and leave their boat to be scuttled.

On this dank and dull morning, Ann pulled out a chair and sat at the table opposite her husband. She reached for his hand and covered it with hers. She kept her voice low, no longer hectoring.

'I know you meant well, a steady job, maybe promotion and not so hard on the body,' she said. 'But it's too dangerous.'

John looked at her. He could feel her concern.

'Look at last night,' his wife said. 'You said there was shooting. You could have been killed. I get so worried. And there's the children ...'

Her voice trailed off. She was determined not to nag. Yet she was at her wits' end; and so weary with eight children and still in her thirties.

Much as she was concerned for her husband's safety, it was the other aspects of being married to a tidewaiter that were weighing her down. The Customs officers lived in the hearts of the communities they were supposed to be policing. If they were diligent in their efforts to prevent smuggling, they were ostracised and persecuted; the alternative was collaboration with the smugglers, an easy life, and a regular supplement to their meagre pay.

It was an easy option that helped the coasts of Wales, and Cornwall, become happy hunting grounds for the likes of Jolly, Furze and Truscott.

Great-great-grandfather Berry eventually had second thoughts about his decision to take HM Customs' commission. But they came only after eight years of service that gradually descended out of control and left his family on the brink of collapse and penury.

Continuously hassled by wife Ann, he eventually returned to the skilled trade of carpenter and joiner – one that was followed by the men of the Berry family for three generations until Wilfred Berkeley Berry, John's great-great-grandson, my own father, cancelled his apprenticeship as a shipwright and took the civil service examination to become a member of HM Customs, the latter-day successors to the tidewaiters of the 1840s.

And thus the wheel turned full circle.

A LONG-STANDING CUSTOM

In far more recent times, in my teenage years, I am standing on a Cornish cliff top. The gale blowing in from the Atlantic would also be storming into my other Celtic ancestral home along the Welsh coast at Milford Haven. It is an intensely black and moonless night, much as it was when smugglers used the dark to evade the tidewaiters and militia four generations ago. Needles of icy rain sting our faces as we seek shelter in the lee of a hand-crafted stone wall. There are few lights showing from the solid stone cottages of the fishing village clinging to the slopes either side of the narrow harbour down below.

We hear the putt-putt of a two-stroke engine somewhere along the rutted, winding track. The beam of a headlight cuts through the darkness, showing the shards of rain are almost horizontal. The motor-cycle slows to a crawl and turns into the lay-by where our car is parked. My father, the chief preventive officer for Cornwall, steps forward and greets the motor-cyclist.

'Evening, Les.'

'Evening, sir. They'll all be indoors tonight.'

Dad agrees. This is not the weather to be tempting the tide and running a small boat into the narrow treacherous coves below. He takes the logbook Les has removed from his pannier bag. He checks the schedule, makes pretence of looking at his wrist watch and appends his signature. All is well; no matter the weather or the time of day, the men of HM Customs continue guarding this inhospitable coastline on foot, pushbike and motor-cycle.

Sadly, my father was never aware that he was a direct descendant of one of the first men to have defended the British coast against illegal imports. It is a lasting regret that I made this discovery well after he had passed on, a hacking cough and wasted body testifying to his lifelong love of nicotine.

There's no doubt that had he known he would have displayed his officer's commission with even greater pride. This document, now hanging framed on my office wall, states:

'He hath the power to enter into any ship, bottom boat or other vessel and also in the daytime with a writ of assistance and taking with him a constable or other public officer … to enter into any house, shop, cellar, warehouse or other place whatsoever within any port or place whatsoever there to make diligent search and in any case of resistance to break open any door, trunk, chest or any package whatsoever for any uncustomed or prohibited goods and the same to seize …'

Jamaica Inn, high on windswept Bodmin Moor. Always eerie and spooky although the smugglers are reputedly long gone

And so it goes on – the flowery bureaucratic language of the early nineteenth century empowering a public servant of the late twentieth century. It seems such an antiquated system to have persisted unchanged into the age of airport body searches, drug lords and international arms smugglers – so olde-worlde and reminiscent of *Masterman Ready*, the *Boy's Own Paper* and the tales of Daphne Du Maurier, a writer who lived and wrote little more than a sailor's curse from where we stood on that storm-tossed night.

Work as a Customs officer has been a job opportunity for career-minded young Englishmen for more than eight hundred years. And the basic job description has changed little since 1275 when Edward I brought in a tax on wool exports to put some much-needed cash into the nation's coffers.

It became a lucrative source of income that soared after the Black Death plague of 1349 reduced the population of England from about four million to 2.5 million in little more than a year. Landowners looking for a less labour-intensive form of agriculture found it in sheep-farming. Land that had been open to all was ditched and hedged and herds of sheep began grazing where serfs had once sweated. Wool production rose dramatically and, with it, the potential tax revenue.

With taxation, there inevitably came tax avoidance and the king recruited the first Customs staff to oversee the system. At first, the small full-time force of Customs officers concentrated on collecting the levies: they had neither the time nor the resources to ensure everyone paid up. It was only when the royal court realised a considerable amount of evasion was occurring that Customs officers became enforcers as well as collectors – a dual role that remains unchanged today.

The monarchs that followed Edward found more and more goods to tax and devised numerous ways to increase the levies. Instead of taxing goods at the source – on the farm, in the mills or warehouses – it was easier to enforce duties and penalties at the places of import and export. With Britain's borders clearly defined by the sea, shipping movements were relatively easy to detect. Sailing times for square-rigged ships depended on wind, weather and the rise and fall of the tide. At low water, boats simply grounded in the mud at the foot of the quay. Trade along the coast was easy to track.

When Edward I created the Customs service, he provided a custom house with a small staff at thirteen points around the coast. To land goods elsewhere needed permission from the authorities at one of these main ports. Customs officers not only had to handle ships entering the official ports but also to maintain a watch over the entire coastline in between. In East Anglia, for example, the Customs officers at Yarmouth had to keep watch on 140 kilometres of coastline, north to Blakeney and south to Woodbridge.

Responsibility for levying the duty rested with a Collector of Customs and his boss, the Controller of Customs. These two were supposed to collect the dues, and sign and seal the relevant receipts and other export documents. As a precaution against dishonesty the port seal was made in two halves, with each official holding a half. All documents had to carry both halves to be legal, and each official was separately accountable for the port's transactions.

Customs officers were poorly paid and the precautions did little to stop them profiting from seizures of smuggled goods or making a charge on every receipt they sealed. They put their seal to blank receipts that a merchant simply filled in with whatever figures suited him. Blank receipts were so commonplace by 1433 that a penalty of three years' jail plus seizure of all belongings was introduced.

Towards the end of the seventeenth century exports from England's southern counties got seriously out of control with an estimated 120,000 packs of wool being exported illegally each year. In the southeastern county of Kent, my birthplace, wool exporters, known as 'owlers', became so determined to evade government levies that hundreds of armed men were eventually involved in each owling venture.

In a bid to stop the rot, Charles II set up the Board of Customs in 1671. By 1685 there were ten smacks patrolling the coast between Yarmouth and Bristol. In 1690, a force of mounted Customs officers – called riding officers – was established. This was something of a misnomer as the so-called 'force' consisted of a mere eight riding officers and was expected to patrol the entire Kent coastline.

A dangerous job – preventive men set upon by smugglers

The riding officers not only had to contend with the owlers, but with a growing tide of smuggled imports. The most recent war with the French had led to a further hoisting of import duties and smugglers found they could now make a profit on both legs of their cross-Channel journey. Ships that went out loaded with wool came back groaning with foreign luxuries.

The shortage of riding officers was recognised in 1698 when the force (now called the Landguard) was expanded, at first to fifty and later to three hundred. Although the concept of a land-based patrol thus became well established the upper hand remained with the sea-borne smugglers who could simply land goods at the point where the preventive effort was weakest. It was left to the navy to oppose the smugglers at sea until, at the turn of the century, a fleet of twenty-one Customs boats (the current Waterguard) was stationed all around the coast to intercept and board ships before they made landfall.

A Surveyor of Customs was appointed at each port to monitor controllers and collectors. As the number of dues increased the service expanded and more officers were introduced. And so another bureaucracy was born.

To thwart the unscheduled offloading of goods, Customs officers began boarding ships down river or well before they neared their anchorage. In London, the tidewaiter joined boats downstream at Greenwich to make sure the cargo was not unloaded on an isolated jetty out of sight of the waiting triumvirate of controller, collector and surveyor (all no doubt eyeing each other suspiciously).

Once a ship had been guided into dock, other staff took over. A coast-waiter supervised the unloading of cargoes from home ports while a land-waiter watched over loading and unloading of boats from foreign ports. A land surveyor kept an eye on both.

Languishing at the bottom of the Customs ladder was another trio of officials: a searcher to check that the ship's cargo tallied with what was on the receipt; a weigher to unpack the cargo and weigh it; and a tidesman or tidewaiter, who stayed with the vessel until the unloading was complete.

These procedures and hierarchies governed great-great-grandfather John Berry's life. Although expanded and refined down the years, they continued to be followed by his great-grandson, my father, a century or so later.

The cliff top patrolmen I came to know as dad checked their schedules in the wildest of weather also lived in their communities like our ancestors in south Wales. Now, however, those they pursued no longer came from within but from without, and they had far more powerful and maneuverable vessels equipped with technology never imagined by their forebears.

The stakes are now far higher, the goods more dangerous. The people involved run their operations from afar by internet, satellite and mobile phone from untraceable locations.

Dad's patrolmen, regardless of how quaint and antiquated they might have appeared, were as effective as when first introduced by King Charles four hundred years earlier. Those intending to glide innocently into Cornwall's coves and harbours probably paid scant attention to a man on a pushbike pedalling along the clifftops. Yet few carriers of contraband escaped those keen eyes. Details of any craft seen straying out of the main shipping lanes soon had its details transmitted up the line and a boarding party was waiting on the quayside when it eventually made landfall.

At other times action was more immediate with the Customs cutter coming alongside way out at sea and delivering a team of eager dungaree-clad searchers who clambered aboard ready to crawl into every corner and crevice to ferret out illicit goods.

Dad relished such moments. It was *Boy's Own Adventure* stuff to him – a man who was forever younger than his years. There was nothing he loved more than getting out from behind his desk and its mounds of paperwork and heading out across Falmouth Bay in the teeth of a gale to clamber up a meagre rope ladder swaying and banging against the side of some suspect ship.

Occasionally, against all the rules and in a way that could never happen in today's over-regulated society, he secreted me aboard the Customs launch to let me share the thrill of the chase – great moments of father-son bonding with a man whose eyes perpetually twinkled with a sense of mischief and adventure.

The most momentous of these occasions came when, for two weeks over Christmas 1951 and into the new year, the attention of the entire world seemed to fall on Falmouth as one of the greatest maritime dramas of modern times was played out in a hurricane 300 miles out in the Atlantic.

Our little town was under the global spotlight. It was rarely off the front page of the world's press for the best part of the following fortnight. All manner of media flooded in and made it their home. And thanks to dad's involvement, I had my first close contact with the daily press and those who write the stories. Being so involved in the adrenalin rush, the pace, the excitement, the ceaseless pursuit of *the* story doubtless combined to provide an early spur that set this then teenage schoolboy on to the path I followed for the rest of my life.

The focal point of all this excitement was the 6700-ton New York-registered cargo ship *Flying Enterprise* carrying forty crew and nine passengers from Hamburg to New York. Its cargo was stated to be of pig iron, coffee and furniture – although there was later speculation that it was really zirconium bound for use in the world's first nuclear submarine, the USS *Nautilus*. As the ship was battered by the worst storm in thirty-five years, it developed a stress fracture across the deckhouse and down one side. Soon, one of its holds had filled with water and it immediately began to list badly.

The ship's captain, 37-year-old Danish-born Kurt Carlsen, radioed for help and two US Navy vessels rushed to the scene. The crew and passengers jumped into the freezing seas and all but one were rescued. But, staying true to the traditions of the sea, Captain Carlsen refused to abandon ship.

And that's when the drama really began with the first papers of the new year featuring the only picture available to them, taken from a Royal Navy observer plane, of the lone captain waving as he clung to the after-deck railing as the ship, its decks awash and the starboard propeller out of water, looked about to be swallowed by the huge seas.

Fortunately, radio communication was still possible and Carlsen reported that although 'a little tired' everything was 'fine and dandy' and he was dining on currant buns, beer and wine.

The following day, as a fresh storm began to develop, a state-of-the-art tugboat, the *Turmoil,* left Falmouth to rendezvous with the *Flying Enterprise*. Despite the horrendous conditions, by January 4 it had drawn up alongside the stricken cargo vessel. After several failed attempts to throw a line across, the tug's first mate, Kenneth Dancy, discarded his life jacket and, trusting to luck and judgement, grabbed the tow rope and leapt across the frothing gap between the rolling ships.

It was an amazing act of derring-do and utter courage that was witnessed only by the two main players and the crew of the *Turmoil*. In the days before satellites, the internet and mobile phones the heroic deed took place the reporters and headline writers had little more to work with than the radio report from the tug and Captain Carlsen – and their vivid imaginations.

But some, as ever, were ahead of the game. The *Daily Express* had booked out the Nansidwell country house hotel. This secluded Grade II listed boutique retreat nestled in woodlands overlooking a small cove. It was a mere six miles or so from the frenzy of Falmouth but access was along narrow winding country lanes. Now in residence were a team of *Express* journalists and communications experts led by star reporter and shipping correspondent Montague Lacey.

'Monty', as he was known, and my father had already crossed paths at some other port, most likely Southampton where both 'worked' the transatlantic liners that provided the main travel link to the US in those days well before mass air travel. He was a recognised name in Fleet Street and would not have got there without cultivating contacts in all the right places.

Dad was therefore someone worth keeping in touch with. The reasoning was clear; regardless how events developed out in the Atlantic, any returning ships or people would first have to be processed by HM Customs.

Which explains why Dad, Mum, sister Judy and myself found ourselves dinner guests of the *Daily Express* at the now defunct Nansidwell Manor House Hotel one memorable evening early in January 1952.

Details of the dining experience, which normally would have been enough of a rarity to amaze and delight this gauche teenager, are but a fuzzy haze on the mind's far horizon. What remains is the frisson of watching Monty and his team not only setting up workable communication with the main players three hundred miles out in the gale-blown Atlantic but also listening to them probe and question to extract the information needed to fully flesh out the bare bones that so much of their opposition were having to cope with.

And in the midst of all the tension and hubbub, Monty found time to chat with a gobsmacked sixteen-year-old still two years away from eschewing all his parents' dreams of him proceeding to university in favour of a three-year apprenticeship as a cadet reporter on the local weekly journal.

To top it off was Monty's revelation that under the same roof were the parents of Captain Carlsen, flown in by the Express from his native Denmark so that they could talk to their son as the drama unfolded. And there was plenty to talk about

With a line attached, tug and stricken vessel were now limping their way towards Falmouth, which was now awash to the gunwales (to borrow an appropriate marine term) with yet more reporters, photographers, film crews and tourists converging on the town to await their arrival.

Suddenly the drama took another twist. Early in the morning of 10 January, a mere forty miles out of Falmouth, the weather worsened and the tow line snapped. The *Flying Enterprise* began rolling so badly her superstructure barely showed above the waves.

A few hours later her stern plummeted, her bows pointed skywards, and within forty minutes she disappeared below the surface. Captain Carlsen and tug man Dancy somehow hauled themselves up the funnel and jumped into the sea to be picked up by the *Turmoil*.

For the journalists waiting in Falmouth the story had just got bigger but they needed to contact the only two men who could tell it.

An immense flotilla of all manner of craft surrounded the *Turmoil* as she eased towards her moorings with Captain Carlsen and second mate Dancy having to be officially processed as foreign 'arrivals'.

Threading it way towards her was the Custom cutter. Dad preparing to do its duty and me alongside him having been sneaked aboard to witness the finale of this dramatic event. The two boats drew level, a ladder lowered for a Customs officer to step aboard and a blur of action as the transfer was made.

Blink. Did I just see what I thought I saw; two bodies, not one?

Dad laid a hand around my shoulder. Said nothing but gave a brief conspiratorial smile. The press had to gather the facts, and he had always been an *Express* reader. Nothing more need be said but sometime later I did get treated by Monty to a personal tour of the shiny black temple that was the Express building in Fleet Street.

And so we move back to Wales and walk again in the footsteps of dad's great-grandfather, tidewaiter John Berry …

A LESSON HARD-EARNED

THE ADVENT OF THE internet and the huge and ever-expanding online resources provided by Ancestry, Find My Past, FreeBMD, Family Search and the like have been a boon to family historians, bringing centuries of invaluable records directly to their desks.

Much more remains stored in record offices, libraries and vast depositories such as the National Archives. It is in such places that researchers can trawl through mountains of cracked and yellowed papers that painstakingly document their ancestors' lives with all their triumphs and misdemeanours minutely recorded.

And it was during a visit I made to the National Archives that I saw my great-great-grandfather, John Berry, change from a mere statistic in the census to a real person with all his struggles and blemishes.

John Berry never allowed his sons to suffer the mistake he had made. His instructions were definite. 'You'll be apprenticed to a good master and learn a decent trade,' he sternly told them as they reached employable age. His dogma was 'don't do as I do but do as I say'.

He had learned a hard lesson when he did what was so rarely done in those days and switched trades and made his move from carpenter and shipwright to tidewaiter. Too late he learned what a bad move it had been.

'It's not so hard on the body,' he had told wife Ann as they discussed his decision. 'And the money is no worse. It will be more secure, too, working for the government.'

How wrong he was, and how much he later regretted being so stubborn.

There may have been an element of security in being a commissioned officer of the Board of Customs. And the job may have appeared physically less demanding than hauling and fixing the timbers used in building Pembroke Dockyard's growing fleet of ships. But, as he soon discovered, the hours were terrible, the constant exposure to an unfriendly climate even worse.

How did he not understand that a tidewaiter's duty hours were governed not by the clock but by the incoming waters? He, and the ships he had to check, waited for the tide to be high before their work could proceed. It was a job for all hours and all weathers. And the weather out on Milford Sound is among the worst of any the Atlantic slams at Britain's western shores.

Too late he realised that the hard labour of a shipwright's daily toil was the lesser evil. And he made sure his sons knew it. One by one they were apprenticed off to the dockyards, signing the onerous indentures that would rule the first three years of their working lives.

Eldest son Douglas was already an apprentice shipwright when John turned up on 15 July 1846 for his first day of duty as one of seventeen commissioned boatmen and tidewaiters based at HM Customs House, Milford Haven, a solid bluestone building that today does service as a harbourside museum of the town's maritime history.

The Customs records give John's age at that time as twenty-seven [i.e. born in 1819, which is at slight variance with the 1841 census, in which he is stated to be twenty-five with an estimated birth year of 1816. It also differs from the 1851 census, which shows him then to be thirty-nine with a birth year of 1812 and almost coincides with church records giving the date of his baptism as 1811! However, early census dates were approximations within five-year time spans].

Milford Custom House where John Berry was based is now an excellent maritime museum

His basic salary was £5.00 plus an allowance of 5s a day when employed as a tidewaiter and reduced to 2s 6d a day when engaged as a boatman. In his first six months, he was described as 'capable and very attentive'. He had ten days' leave and no absences through illness or for other reasons.

All this is recorded in the annual records of the Comptroller and Collector for the port of Milford, wordily subtitled as: *An account of the names, ages, capacities and conduct of the several officers belonging to this post for the year ending 5 January 1847.*

Similar details follow year by year up to John Berry's departure from the service in October 1857. His enforced departure occurred after a series of misdemeanours that seem out of character considering that, until that year, his conduct had been consistently recorded as 'capable and attentive' or similar. For 1848 he was described as 'capable and very attentive' and again in 1849, when he also took four days leave.

In 1850 he was 'active and attentive' with 'regular attendance' and enjoyed fourteen days leave. The following year, although he was again written up as 'capable and attentive' he was also shown to have taken a somewhat surprising twenty-four days of leave. Surely no worker in the mid-nineteenth century ever enjoyed the extreme luxury of such a long absence from their daily grind. Other factors must have been the cause.

And so it proved as on almost the first page I turned to in *The Output Records from the Collector of Customs at Milford Haven* one heading leapt out at me:

13 May 1851
Berry charged

Beneath, in neat copperplate handwriting, Collector of Customs W Hodgson records that at ten o'clock the previous night 'John Berry, one of the tidewaiters at the port, was found ... absent from his vessel'.

He should have been on board the *Mecca*, which had arrived from Cuba with a cargo of mahogany. He was severely reprimanded, but only 'as a precautionary (measure)'. He was also cautioned 'to be more circumspect in his duty for the future' and ordered that 'he should not be boarded as a tidewaiter for a month' – which explains those twenty-four days of so-called 'leave' which were, in reality, suspension from all duties.

This would have meant reduced pay, enforced time at home in the cramped cottage with Ann and their nine children and probably a few sessions at one of the numerous local hostelries knocking back the odd tankard of ale or three. Or maybe, thanks to his close connections with the smuggling trade, a few noggins of duty-free rum. After all, as later records were to show, he was not averse to hitting the bottle, which would scarcely have found favour with his already embittered wife.

This record of his absenteeism contains fully documented details of charges against officers of HM Customs from September 1816 through to January 1876. They include orders from the Board of Customs to its Milford Haven collector, letters from the collector to the board, miscellaneous notes and correspondence and even some wreck disposal records.

Despite being reprimanded, cautioned and removed from duty in May 1851, John Berry was back in collector Hodgson's bad books a mere three months later with a repeat performance:

26 August 1851
John Berry charged

The collector's report is brief:

'John Berry, one of the tidewaiters at the port, was brought up before me on account of his having been absent from his watch on the morning of the 24th inst when boarding on the *Sophia* (master: William Marten from Quebec)'.

Once again, great-great-granddad was reprimanded and cautioned to be more circumspect in future.

Maybe the reprimand had an effect. The year-end report for 1852 continues to describe him as 'capable and attentive'. However, it also notes he took three sick days as well as another three days off for 'other causes'. Alongside this latter entry is written the comment 'suspected of being intoxicated', which makes one wonder how often he sought solace in the bottle or the pub.

There followed three years in which John was variously credited as being 'a very good officer' (1853), 'capable and generally attentive' (1854) and 'generally attentive and capable' (1855). However, there was another unexplained batch of twenty-two days leave in 1853 that raises doubts about his attendance record and the reason for such a lengthy absence in view of his earlier record.

A suggestion that he was gradually sliding into bad ways comes from the original 1854 entry stating him to be an 'attentive and good officer'. This was later ruled through and replaced by a somewhat lesser and more general commendation. He is downgraded from 'attentive' to merely 'capable', and from being 'a good officer' to one who is 'generally attentive'. All of which seems justified by what occurs in subsequent years.

It was in 1856 when the rot really set in and John Berry's tidewaiter duties began to weigh heavy on him.

Supervising the tidewaiters was tide surveyor Thomas Landells. Born in Sunderland, Landells came all the way south to Pembrokeshire in 1849 and moved with his pregnant wife Mary and their five children into a house in Front Street, Steynton (later part of Milford). The salary gap between his position and that of a tidewaiter is evident not only from the 'better' address but also the fact that the Landells' household included a servant, Luisa Jenkins.

Overseeing Landells, was tide surveyor Henry Sutherst, another northerner – from Liverpool. It was he who, on 9 October 1856, levelled two charges against the increasingly delinquent tidewaiter John Berry.

The first was that 'whilst boarded upon the *Henry Holman* during the last month Berry demanded and received from the master of that ship a pecuniary reward for the performance of his duty'. In other words, he allegedly took a bribe, probably to look the other way while contraband was offloaded.

The second charge was that on 7 October 1856 my increasingly negligent ancestor 'absented himself from the ship *Hercules* at Pembroke Dock upon which he was boarded, leaving his duty wholly unprovided for'. This immediately arouses the suspicion that the absence was more than accidental or a case of bunking off for bite to eat or, more likely, a cheering ale. The connection to that other charge of accepting 'a pecuniary reward' is easy to make.

All the more so when, on 25 October 1856, the Board of Customs, sitting in faraway London, gives priority to finding him guilty on the second count and then *also* considers him 'very reprehensible in receiving money from the ship's husband under any pretext'.

Wife Ann's mood was as dark and unforgiving as the

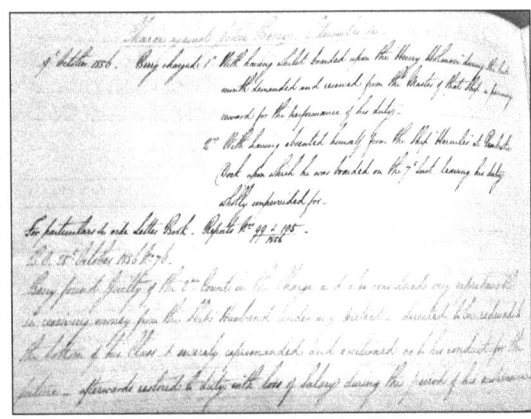

John Berry charged by HM Customs [a document from the National Archives]

dreary wintry weather when he arrived home that evening at the tiny cottage at the end of the village bordering Pill Creek. She gave him scant time to push his way through the door and bend to remove his muddy boots.

'Well?'

Seven of their children were clustered around her. All eyes were fixed on him. It was more unnerving and harder to take than standing before the comptroller and the surveyor.

'I suppose you've been skulking in the Heart of Oak. Or was it the Lord Nelson?'

John nodded sheepishly without saying a word. It mattered little to specify which of the town's many pubs he had stopped off in; the deed itself was enough to increase his guilt. But he hadn't lingered; there was no money to spare for beer. And there would be even less now.

He mumbled words that Ann assumed were some sort of apology, or excuse.

'I needed something,' John added. 'Only a tot.'

'Hah,' Ann scoffed. 'Can't face us without the rum in your belly, is that it? Then it's bad news. Come on, let's get it over and done. Best we know what's in store.'

She sat at the table – poorly-matched planks of timber resting on scavenged tea chests. The children gathered closer. John looked at them: a judge and her jury. It was worse than he had faced down at the Customs House only a few hours earlier.

'Reprimanded,' said John. Best to ease his way in, give them the good news first.

Ann's stare did not waver. She knew there was more and her look was as good as a prompt.

John took the hint. 'Cautioned,' he added. 'About my future conduct, they said.'

'And?'

'Demoted. Reduced to the bottom of my grade and suspended from duty.'

John watched his wife's head droop, resting in upturned hands, long black hair trailing forward. No sound, no movement apart from one big upheaval of her shoulders; a massive sigh before she slowly raised her head and again fixed him with that stare. John shuffled his feet, uneasy and wilting.

'That's not all, is it?' said Ann.

He shuffled forward, leaned over the table and held her hands.

'It's only a suspension … I'll be going back.'

Suddenly she stood, thrusting his hands away, pushing her hair back from her brow, all semblance of calm now gone, replaced by a fury John had come to know all too well. She spat her words at him.

'But that's not all, is it, you stupid man? It's not only the suspension. Suspension means no money, nothing coming in for food and everything else. How can you do this to us?'

John had no answer. The verdict handed to him that afternoon had spelt it out: he would be restored to duty but with loss of salary during the seventeen days of his suspension.

There was little domestic harmony in the last cottage at the end of the village of Coomb on Pill Creek that night.

The 1856 year-end report shows that in the few weeks following his suspension and return to duty, John Berry had been 'very attentive and an efficient officer'. But within six months things began going downhill in a very big way.

At 10pm on 12 May 1857 the tide surveyor found Berry absent from duty on the vessel on which he had been boarded, and again the ship is the *Mecca,* the scene of his first infraction some years previously. Again, he was severely reprimanded by the Comptroller and Controller and cautioned to be more circumspect in his duty in future. He was removed from tidewaiter boarding duty for a whole month.

Neither the reprimand nor the suspension had much effect as on 24 August 1857 he was again found absent from his watch when boarded on the *Sophia* which had arrived from Quebec. For this repeat 'dereliction of duty' he was once more reprimanded and cautioned to be more circumspect in future. It is later recorded that neither of these incidents nor 'several' other cases were submitted to the Board of Customs for its consideration but were dealt with locally.

Among these other cases was one that shone a light into the world beyond his work and highlighted the dire straits being endured on the home front. On 14 October 1857 John Berry was arrested on the vessel on which he was boarded 'for arrears of rent on his dwelling house'. He was immediately sent to gaol but gained an early release after somehow coming to an arrangement with his creditors.

On 31 October 1857, the board ordered that he be returned to duty with loss of seventeen days pay during his suspension. Such a penalty only exacerbated the situation he and Ann faced. Being suspended meant being on minimum or no pay – so it became an even harder task to comply with the board's demand that he liquidate his debts and avoid involving himself in 'pecuniary liabilities which you may be unable to meet'.

Despite this woeful succession of misdemeanours, the Collector's year-end report for 1857 somehow manages to look on the bright side and describes great-great-grandfather's conduct as 'capable and attentive'.

But after making an untroubled start to 1858 and enjoying several months free of any charges being laid against him, the wheels well and truly came off John Berry's career in HM Customs, The downhill slide began on the evening of 5 September when tide surveyor Henry Sutherst visited 'the vessels of charge' in Pembroke Dock and 'found John Berry, commissioned tidewaiter, absent from the *Sarah*, which had recently arrived from Quebec'.

Sutherst reported that John Berry had left the vessel in the charge of his partner, J M Davies, 'who was on watch and attentive'.

The Collector and Comptroller of HM Customs not only ordered great-great-grandpa John to report the cause of his absence but also noted that he had been seen 'in a boat with others proceeding down the harbour'. But John Berry reckoned he had good reason, as stated in his written explanation:

> *Gent'm: In answer to the above charge I have to state on Saturday 5.30 pm I received a message informing me that one of my family lay very ill and if I wished to see her alive I must immediately come home. Having a parent's feeling and knowing I could not see the tide surveyor to ask for leave I left the vessel in charge of my partner for a few hours expecting to be back in time for my own watch which commenced at midnight, but unfortunately my child getting worse I could not. I remained home on Sunday until late in the evening*

having four miles to walk and a ferry to cross I could not obtain
a boat. In consequence, I was obliged to remain until early in the
morning when I got on board before the hours of working. Gentm,
I beg to state that the vessel was not left unguarded by my partner
being in charge during my absence and under the circumstances I
beg for your clemency. I remain &c, J Berry.

The Collector and Comptroller was not convinced. An air of disbelief hangs over his 20 September 1858 letter in which he directed John Berry 'to produce a certificate from the medical officer in attendance upon his child in corroboration of the dangerous situation which he states to have been in at the time of his absence'.

But his doubts were unfounded as a note written on 30 September 1858 by Milford doctor Richard H Byers, MRCP, confirmed that '*John Berry applied to me some time since for medicine for one of his children, which I gave him but do not remember the date*'.

Unfortunately, the authorities were not prepared to let the matter rest. On 4 October 1858 they served notice on 'John Berry, tidewaiter and boatman' that:

> *We hereby charge you with having been absent from the vessel*
> *upon which you were boarded on the evening of the 5th ultimo at*
> *8.50, the hour at which the tide surveyor visited the Sarah, out of*
> *Quebec. To which matter you are required to make a plain and*
> *distinct answer in writing on or before the 8th proximo taking care*
> *to avoid all scurrilous or abusive expressions. HP & HS*

'That's unfair, unjust,' railed John Berry as he and Ann fumed over his bosses' refusal to accept his explanation.

'Where's the compassion for a man who is sick with worry over a child he fears might die?' queried Ann, this time fully supportive of her husband.

John Berry wasted little time in replying, nor any effort in drafting a different or stronger explanation. He looked at Ann, forlorn and helpless, his hands spread wide in despair.

'Those are the facts, what more can I say?'

Little wonder that the letter he obediently delivered on 7 October was almost identical to his earlier statement.

At a formal hearing that followed, tide surveyor Henry Sutherst made a sworn statement about the events on the evening of 5 September during his rounds of the vessels berthed and waiting to be unloaded. Among them was the *Sarah*, moored off Pater, a part of Pembroke, discharging a cargo of wood goods.

Sutherst said John Berry had been boarded on the *Sarah* on 28 August and was joined by J M Davies, a fellow commissioned tidewaiter, on 30 August. When Sutherst asked about John Berry's whereabouts, Davies told him that, '*He was not on board, that he had not returned from his leave.*'

Sutherst added. '*I had given Berry leave to be absent from the vessel from 6 am to noon on this day being Sunday. After visiting some other vessels, I returned to the Sarah about 10 pm and asked Davies whether Berry had returned. He said 'No'. I reported the case to the Collector the following morning'.*

John Berry was clearly resigned to his fate for he declined an offer to question Sutherst. He took a similar line even when his colleague, J M Davies, gave evidence that seems to support his plea.

John Mitchell Davies joined the service on 7 September 1857 on probation as a tidewaiter and boatman at Milford. He appears to have been continually employed in this capacity, without a blemish on his record, until sometime in 1868. He told the hearing,

> *About 5.30 pm on Saturday the 4th my partner John Berry. told me that he had received a message from home stating that some of his family were ill and that he should go hence and should return on the following afternoon and requested me to keep a good lookout in his absence.*

Davies also supported Sutherst's record of events and added that John Berry had eventually returned to the vessel about 6 am on Monday 6 September.

He also provided the information that before John Berry had left the ship on Saturday, '*A person came to the vessel and had a conversation with him*'.

Again, John Berry offered no comment on the evidence and called no witnesses on his behalf. There is a sense from the report of these proceedings that he had given up and decided there was nothing he could say or do to change his superiors' minds. He was resigned to whatever verdict was passed.

The reports of these proceedings in Milford were forwarded to the Board of Customs in London on 11 October 1858, claiming *it requisite a charge of dereliction of duty be preferred against John Berry, commissioned tidewaiter at the port.*

The documents presented to the board said John Berry's action arose from a message *he allegedly received from his home necessitating he return in consequence of severe domestic affliction.*

Although his superiors admitted being informed that some of Berry's family *have been suffering from the epidemic so prevalent in the county during the past season ... we cannot ascertain that any sickness of a dangerous character itself in connection with his statement.*

A damning final paragraph as good as sealed John Berry's fate:

> *The case in our opinion has arisen from the characteristic indifference so frequently displayed by this class of officer at the port towards the wellbeing of the public service and is deserving of punishment.*

It comes as no surprise to read in the Board of Customs bulletin No.33 for 1858 that great-great-grandfather John Berry was found guilty of these latest charges. It also considered the former instances of misconduct laid against him and declared him to be, '*an unfit person to be retained in this service*'.

The board directed that he be dismissed.

Thus his career with HM Customs came to an ignominious and sudden end and it was left to his great-grandson, my father Wilfred Berkeley Berry, to set about restoring the family's good name within the service when he gave up a dockyard career and accepted HM Customs' commission on 30 April 1930.

John Berry took the reverse route and went back to life as a shipwright and joiner, the trade my father later forsook, and saw family and workaday life take a considerable turn for the better. This improvement in their circumstances was accompanied by an inevitable feeling of smug satisfaction on hearing that Henry Sutherst had been demoted to tidewaiter and transferred to another port for being drunk on duty.

Until then, Sutherst and his family had lived comfortably at 13 Marine Gardens, the small row of harbourside houses on the undercroft below the prestigious Hamilton Terrace, a far cry from the Berrys' own tiny damp cottage at Coomb. It had further rankled John to learn when colleague

John Davies was giving evidence about his absence from duty that Davies also not only lived in the more salubrious Marine Gardens, but at No. 12, right next door to the Suthersts.

How cosy was that?

But fortune's wheel kept turning turn and by 1871 John Berry and his family had also moved into Marine Gardens, two doors along from the shipbuilding yard nestled next to the toll house and the pier (with its resident pier-keeper).

John Davies was still at No. 12 but by then, at the young age of 33, he was a widower and living as a lodger.

THE BOY NEXT DOOR

By the time John Berry had overcome his troublesome years as a tide-waiter and his dismissal from HM Customs and returned to his former trade as a joiner and cabinetmaker – as wife Ann had long urged him to do - daughter Agness was not only a fully-qualified dressmaker but had married Thomas Nicholas and thus become what was officially described as a Trinity House seaman's wife.

And thus was formed the union from which my Cornish links are descended.

Agness was a dressmaker's apprentice when she met Thomas, a sturdy young mariner living a few doors further along Middle Street from where she lodged with her grandparents, Joseph Berry (my 3x great-grandfather) and his wife Margaret (nee Bevans).

Like many of the Berry clan, Joseph was a cabinet maker and carpenter and was doing well enough for he and Margaret to employ a live-in servant girl to help with chores and look after their two other lodgers, magistrate's gentleman William Corzens and his magistrate's clerk son, Charles. When Joseph's son, Thomas Benjamin Warlow Berry, took over the business after his father's death in 1860, it was employing five boys.

Milford had grown into a thriving waterside township of solid businesses, skilled artisans and an overall air of prosperity – a far cry from the rather sad and down-at-heel main street of today with its boarded-up shops, vacant premises and high unemployment. It sits forlorn and almost forgotten only a few steps up the slope from where a glittering marina lies crammed with luxurious craft that mostly cost more than a home in the neighbouring streets. Such a contrast in affluence and aspiration.

The Nicholas family of the early 1800s belonged to that other solid sector of the rapidly expanding Milford community that derived its livelihood from all things marine. When Agness met Thomas his father, James, was still serving as a gunner on a Royal Navy cutter patrolling the Milford

Haven harbour and the wilder waters beyond. In the following years he took less arduous duties as a boatswain aboard a revenue cutter.

In June 1868, Thomas's younger brother, Charles, joined Trinity House, the body responsible for maintaining the lighthouses and lightships that provide a ring of safety around the English and Welsh coasts. He served in at least eight lighthouses and was still listed as a principal keeper when living in retirement in East Ham, London, in 1911. For seven years (1894-1901) he was keeper of the Trevose Head light on the Cornish north coast just south of the now trendy fishing port of Padstow – yet another of my links between the Celtic nations.

It was no surprise, therefore, that Thomas decided to follow in the footsteps of his father and his brother, enlisting in the merchant marine in his late teens as a general seaman and sometime later joining Trinity House. Soon after, he apparently also found religion and became a seamen's missionary.

One of Thomas's earliest postings – before his marriage to Agness – was to the frequently storm-tossed lightship *Helwick*, anchored off the Welsh coast at Mumbles, close to Swansea. There he was one of seven crew – the master, two lamplighters, three ordinary seamen and a carpenter – living in the most cramped conditions imaginable and with their 'home' continually tossed from side to side, from wave to wave.

A painting of the Helwick Lightship

The lightship marks the treacherous sands off the western point of the Mumbles Peninsular, close to the entrance to the Bristol Channel, and is fully exposed to all that the Atlantic seas can hurl at it. These were (and still are) tempestuous and dangerous waters and the *Helwick*'s crews played a pivotal role on the frequent occasions when ships were in strife or ran aground.

There has been a succession of lightships named *Helwick* but only the more recent vessels have been preserved. One of these is moored in Cardiff, open to the public all year round and serving as a Christian Fellowship centre, a neat link back to when Thomas Nicholas converted from ordinary seaman to seamen's missionary to provide help and solace to those, like him, who had endured time on the *Helwick*.

Exactly when he saw the light is uncertain. Maybe it was no sudden blinding flash of divine intervention but a gradual conversion. He states his occupation as a seaman in the merchant service on the register for his marriage to Agness in the Haverfordwest Register Office on 14 August 1858 and is listed in the 1861 census simply as an able-bodied seaman aboard the *Helwick*.

But by the time of the 1871 census, his employment was no longer in doubt. He and Agness and their five children were then living in Robert Street next door to Agness's brother, John, and his wife Emily, and his occupation was given as seaman's missionary ... and dressmaker Agness was listed as a seaman's missionary's wife.

Thomas was the eldest of five children born to James Nicholas and wife Ann (nee Lewis) – and was surrounded by people for whom the sea was their life. James, had served as a gunner on a Royal Navy cutter patrolling the Welsh coast and at the time of his death at Milford on 22 January 1868, aged 72, he was recorded in the *Pembrokeshire Herald* as being chief officer of the RC *Skylark*.

The family's neighbours were predominantly lighthouse keepers, ship-wrights, mariners or dockyard workers.

[These discoveries of ancestors who spent their lives in sea-washed communities and marine occupations perhaps explain the pull I have always felt towards waterside living. Rarely have I lived away from easy sight of the sea. Yet, until these recent explorations into my past, I never understood why. Simply, it seems, it is in the blood – the blood of generations of coastal dwellers I never knew existed].

The date of Agness and Thomas's wedding suggests it was a matter of 'doing the right thing' and was planned in haste as their first child, Douglas James, was born the following April.

Almost two years later –while Thomas was away from home being tossed around by the rough seas of Swansea Bay aboard the *Helwick* – Douglas was joined by Charles Edwin, the brother who eventually followed their father into the lighthouse service and forged the Berry family's link between Wales and Cornwall.

Over the next seventeen years, Agness produced five daughters and two more sons, their births coming with almost predictable regularity every two to three years. By the time of the arrival of the last, daughter

Ethel in 1878, she was forty-two with seven of her brood still living in their small house on Robert Street, a few doors away from the family of my great-great-grandfather, John Berry, and conveniently sited next door to the Tabernacle Chapel.

The two who had fled the coop were Agnes (without her mum's double s to her name), married to a Salvation Army captain, and my cousin Charles, already moving from lighthouse to lighthouse around the British coast.

With a seagoing father, a naval gunner grandfather, a lighthouse-keeper for an uncle and the ever-busy harbour a mere hundred-yard dash down the hill from home, it is little wonder that at the age of eighteen cousin Charles had enrolled in the service of Trinity House.

After initial training, he was appointed in 1881 as a supernumery keeper at the light on the long sandy spit overlooking the Humber estuary at Spurn Head. It is hard to imagine a rougher introduction to lighthouse life, especially for a teenager used to the verdant and rugged Pembrokeshire coast.

For centuries, the low-lying three-mile long spit of sand and shingle has been battered and worn away by North Sea tides and storms to the extent that where Charles once worked, and harbourside villages existed in the Middle Ages, is today no longer part of the mainland but an island and wildlife sanctuary.

A succession of lights has been sited there since the seventeenth century but all that remains are the deserted low light (now a water tower) deactivated in 1895 and a disused tower light built in 1895 and discontinued in 1985.

Charles was headed to an earlier twenty-seven-metre tower light. It had been in use since 1767 when John Smeaton was commissioned to build a new pair of lighthouses, one high and one low. But cracks were beginning to appear in the tower, caused by the same tidal erosion that was eating into the surrounding sandbanks. A replacement was called for but by the time that began operating Charles had well and truly moved on. However, the black and white tower where he worked still stands proud on the headland awaiting restoration as a wildlife visitor centre.

Within less than a year spent at Spurn, Charles spent a brief period as assistant keeper at Dungeness, another exposed shore-based light set among miles of shingle on Kent's Channel coast, before returning to his homeland with a posting as an assistant keeper at the Skerries lighthouse, set on a perilous outcrop of rocks close to Holyhead off the northern Welsh isle of Anglesey.

The Skerries light was originally privately owned and first lit in 1716. It was rebuilt around 1759 to a height of 8.5 metres by the owner's heirs for about £3000 and lit by a coal brazier on top of the tower. Morgan Jones, who inherited the lighthouse in 1778, raised the top of the tower by 6.7 metres and built an iron balcony with railings enclosing an oil-burning lantern.

Despite the 1836 Act of Parliament empowering Trinity House to purchase all private lighthouses, it took five years of fighting with the owners to eventually gain possession at a cost of close to £500,000, the last privately owned lighthouse in the British Isles to be bought by Trinity House.

The lighthouse was converted to automatic operation in 1987 and is now monitored and controlled from the Trinity House planning centre in Harwich, Essex.

Charles continued moving from one exposed and barren coastal outpost to another. From 1882 until 1885 he endured three years of spasmodic isolation at the Wolf Rock light, set in the Atlantic Ocean midway between Land's End and the Scilly Isles – his first contact with Cornwall.

It was while stationed at Wolf Rock and living in Penzance that he met and wooed Cornish lass Mary Ann Sidonia Jose. On her father's

Mary Ann Sidonia Jose
[courtesy Heather Williams]

side, Sidonia came from a long-established family of Lizard area serpentine miners and stone carvers. Her mother was a Gilbert, two of whose relatives went off to fight in the Great War and never came back but whose names are honoured on the war memorial alongside the parish church in the often storm-bludgeoned old fishing village of Mullion.

Sidonia and Charles were married in Landewednack Parish Church on 20 November 1883. According to a report in *The Cornishman*, the Reverend P V Robinson conducted the wedding ceremony 'in a very impressive manner'.

Twenty-one-year-old Sidonia, the name by which I always think of her, was 'tastefully dressed in peacock blue silk, trimmed with bruche silk to match'.

It indeed sounds most 'impressive' and suggests there was no lack of money among the two families, especially as the 'much esteemed' bride was also wearing 'a beautiful gold necklet and locket set with diamonds, the present of the bridegroom'.

That this daughter of a cutter and polisher of the area's unique serpentine stone lived at the Lizard, quite a journey from Penzance, suggests young Charles must have had some relief from the isolation of Wolf Rock and may even have spent time at the shore-based Lizard lighthouse (and in the nearby Jose household) before being officially posted there in 1885, two years after their marriage.

For the first four years of married life, the couple lived at Sidonia's family home in Green Cottage, which still stands in a dominant position facing the somewhat desolate village green at Landewednack. In that time, Sidonia gave birth to Percival Thomas on 31 January 1885 and Francis Norman on 31 December the same year.

Then followed five tragic years in which there were three more births with none of the children surviving more than a few months. The couple's first daughter, Irena Teva Jose, was born in April 1887 but died at the very start of 1888. Charles Wesley, born in 1890 and no doubt named after the firebrand Methodist preacher who could draw crowds akin to those lured by modern pop stars, lived only twenty-three days before succumbing to a haemorrhaging of the bowel on 2 December 1890.

Charles Claude was born on 20 March 1892 and baptised on 28 March but tragedy struck again and on 22 April, he died from 'marasmus, severe malnutrition resulting in energy deficiency' and a body weight less than sixty per cent of the norm.

Noticeably, the death certificate records it was grandfather Francis Jose who was 'present at the death' of Charles Wesley rather than the tot's father, who can only be assumed to have been far away and on duty when his son died.

In 1899, Charles had been reappointed to Dungeness, the light set on the bleak shingled English Channel shores at Lydd. His son's funeral was hardly over before the family made the long journey to their new quarters here on the edge of Kent's permanently windswept Romney Marshes. The grieving mother at least had some comforting female companionship and help with household chores from Charles' sister, school governess Ada, who decided to join them in the keepers' cottages that remain huddled around the base of the lighthouse.

Sidonia decided to leave Dungeness and return to the comfort and care of her Cornish home in Landewednack for the birth (and baptism) of Charles Claude but one cannot help wondering if all the travelling and spartan living contributed in some degree to the newborn's malnutrition, energy deficiency and low body weight.

The gloom cast by these events was further deepened by the absence of Charles, who seems to have remained in Dungeness throughout the birth, death and burial of his son until, in April 1892, there is the stark announcement by Trinity House that, while stationed at Dungeness, 'Nicholas left to join the Hong Kong Lighthouse Services '. There were none of the usual mentions of his duties or his family situation.

After that came a huge gap in all available records. He vanished from the census although wife Sidonia remained and continued giving birth. It was not until 8 April 1930, that a Charles Edward Nicholas reappeared in the records, listed as having died in, of all places, the Hertfordshire town of St Albans. This was so remote from Wales, Cornwall and Hong Kong and the coasts where Charles had spent his entire working life, that it seemed unlikely to be the same man.

But, as further checking proved, together with a death certificate showing his wife as the ever-loyal Mary Ann Sidonia, this was indeed cousin Charles. And later contacts, proved this beyond all doubt and opened yet more windows into my Cornish-Welsh heritage.

As tellers of mystery tales would have it, the plot had thickened. But first, an interlude among my other Celtic kinfolk…

A SCOTTISH INJECTION TO THE CELTIC MIX

SIX TERRITORIES ARE CONSIDERED as Celtic nations. These were developed from the numerous random clans that were such a feature of their earliest days. Collectively, they are known as the Celtic fringe and in each a Celtic language is still spoken to varying degrees.

So far, I have found no direct family links to three of them - Brittany (Celtic name, Breizh), Ireland (Éire) and the Isle of Man (Mannin or Ellan Vannin).

But the Berry connections are strong and direct to the other three - Cornwall (Kernow), Wales (Cymru) and Scotland (Alba).

The major trunk of the ancestral tree is rooted firm and deep in the wild westernmost corner of Wales (with its strong similarities to Cornwall) through the births in Milford of my great-great-grandfather John Berry and his son, great-grandfather Alfred Jabez Berry. However, a brief and sudden

Great-grandfather Alfred Jabez Berry and unknown grandson

change of direction resulted in my grandfather, Alfred Berkeley Berry, being born on the banks of the Clyde.

A Scot!

Reinforcing this Celtic connection north of the border, are his three brothers and a sister born during the family's Clydebank interlude. Two of the brothers, both named Edwin, died in infancy and soon the family returned to be among their Milford kinfolk where they extended the Berry brood with almost clockwork regularity.

Their detour north of the border lasted less than ten years but it gave me three close Scottish ancestors – a great-grandfather, a great-uncle and a great-aunt.

Bring out the bagpipes, don the tartan! *Scots wha hae …*

To great-grandfather Alfred Jabez Berry there was only one solution. But breaking the news to wife Annie was not going to be easy. He took his time walking up the slope from the ferry to the family home on Hamilton Terrace in Milford Haven; he needed to plan and rehearse his words.

He needn't have bothered. Annie knew all was not well the moment he pushed open the door and bent his head beneath the low lintel. His movements were too slow and tentative and the look on his grimy, weather-beaten face did little to dispel any doubts. Her first fears were that there had been accident; someone else they knew had been maimed, even killed, as they laboured on the slipway. It happened too often. There was so little protection for men sawing, chopping, carving and planing too close together in such confined space. Sharp tools, relentless deadlines and demanding bosses were a fatal mix.

She gave him no chance to compose his words. Not even waiting for him to sit on the kitchen chair and unlace his heavy boots.

'What's happened? What's wrong?'

He shrugged, almost relieved he didn't have to pussyfoot around deciding what to say.

'There's no work. We've got to move.'

There, he'd said it. No long explanations.

'What do you mean, move?'

'There's work up in Scotland. On the Clyde. They say they're looking for people like me. They reckon they need my skills, that I can perhaps teach them a thing or two. Maybe not for good, but for a while or so.'

'Scotland!'

Annie was aghast. It was unthinkable. Unimaginable. Near neighbour England was a foreign country to most Welsh people. But Scotland was beyond foreign; a place Annie had heard about but of which she knew next to nothing. Her family, the Lloyds, had lived in Wales for generations. Alfred's family was the same. Except for Annie's uncle, David Lloyd, who migrated to the USA, none had ever ventured more than a few miles in any direction. She and Alfred had gone to the same school; their families lived only a few houses apart. And now he expected her to pack everything up and move far away from all she had ever known.

'What's wrong with staying here?' she asked. 'This is our home. Everyone we know is here, not hundreds of miles away in Scotland. Anyway, where would we live?'

'Seems they're so desperate for workers that they're building homes for them to live in. And right close to the docks, too. It's the only way, love; there'll be no work here soon and we can't live on nothing.'

Annie knew the truth of everything her husband was saying; but it was not what she wanted to hear. It was little more than a year since he had walked her down the aisle after their wedding at the parish church at Steynton and they had yet to start a family. This, however, was more than likely to change, and soon too if past events were anything to go by. She was one of six children and Alfred was one of ten. Big families were the norm, despite the high number of deaths in childbirth and infancy.

'But things will change,' she argued. 'They have before.'

Alfred shrugged, wanting to share her optimism but knowing what the talk was like down on the docks. Most of Pembroke depended in one way or another on the dockyard but it was the Lords Commissioners of the Admiralty far away in London who decided how it was run. The locals had regularly petitioned their lordships to let Pembroke fit out ships completely rather than merely build the hulls. But the Admiralty steadfastly ignored these pleas. It had been a precarious see-sawing existence for the people of Pembroke Dockyard ever since Lord Nelson of Trafalgar fame had encouraged the port's expansion and none were more aware of this than the men who laboured in its sheds and slipways.

'We're in the wrong trade,' said Alfred.

Annie frowned. His words made no sense. Her husband and most of his brothers had done their time as apprentices, learned their trade and were an essential part of what Pembroke did best – build ships. How could he be in the wrong trade?

'We work with wood, not iron.' Alfred spread his hands wide. 'It's as simple as that. They're saying there'll soon be no more timber ships.'

'Who's saying? People spreading rumours, I'll warrant. Haven't you anything better to do than listen to lots of idle gossip?'

She was fired up and angry, irked by the seriousness of her husband's demeanour, how he seemed to have really thought about things before making his announcement. She was in shock at the idea of leaving friends and family.

Alfred put a comforting arm around her shoulder. 'I'm sorry, Annie, but it's all true. The first iron warship has already been launched, the *Warrior*, up at Blackwall on the Thames.'

'Hah, an iron ship,' she scoffed. 'How do they expect it to float?'

'Just like a wooden one,' he said. 'And it's tougher, won't catch fire so easily or be damaged by gunfire.'

The evolution of the iron warship had left the Admiralty with a number of problems. Suddenly almost every major warship in service had become obsolete. France was already building a series of ironclads (timber ships sheathed with iron armour). It was the emergence of these ships, plus a shaky relationship between the two countries, that had finally spurred the Admiralty to change to iron construction. *Warrior* and her sister ship, the *Black Prince*, being all iron, were superior to their French contemporaries but the British shipyards did not have the capacity to match the French program 'keel for keel'.

The Admiralty therefore decided that the design of certain timber ships under construction should be modified drastically and be completed as ironclads. Three such vessels were built at Pembroke and on Thursday June 26, 1862, a Miss Jones of Pantglasl, described as 'a

The Royal Oak, one of the first ironclad frigates

Carmarthenshire lady' performed the ceremony when the yard launched its first iron-cased warship, the *Prince Consort*. Three more interim ironclads followed, the *Research*, the *Zealous* and the *Lord Clyde*.

While these hybrids were being completed, the Admiralty was considering the future of Pembroke Dockyard and what it found did not look promising. The yard was not well suited for building the ships of the new era. There was a small coalfield nearby but it produced anthracite, not good steam coal. Iron works were far distant. The numerous slipways built in earlier years for seasoning the timber hulls were no longer an asset. Pembroke, once the most modern of shipyards, was becoming as obsolescent as the ships it had proudly built.

Elsewhere in Britain there were already commercial shipyards skilled in working with the new material; they were usually adjacent to coalfields, ironworks and engine builders, often all belonging to the same company or ironmaster. Pembroke shipwrights and carpenters such as the men of the Berry family did not know much about iron, and probably did not want to know. As they worked on the *Lord Clyde* they feared it would be the last, or almost the last, wooden capital ship to be built.

'Better make it a good one,' John Berry said to his sons. 'Give them something to remember us by.'

'Not so sure about that,' said eldest son Douglas. 'It's more like a wake than something we should be celebrating.'

His brother, John, agreed.

'I'll do as good a job as ever, but I can't say I can get up much enthusiasm. Where's the pride in having all your work hidden by sheets of iron? My heart's not in it.'

Alfred said nothing but listened intently to his father and his brothers. He was newly apprenticed to the dockyard and bound by strict terms of employment that allowed no scope for dissent or opinions. Nonetheless he could not help but wonder what the future held. Where was the sense in learning all the skills needed to work with timber when the future seemed to be one of hammering metal rivets and bending sheets of iron? Even if the future of the yard was less gloomy than his brothers were predicting it was obvious there would be much less need for workers in wood.

No sooner had the *Lord Clyde* been launched than the word went around the yard that the Government was considering closing the royal dockyards at Deptford, Woolwich, Sheerness and Pembroke. The radical proposal was given strength by reports that the *Lord Clyde* was proving to be something of a disaster. Not only were her main engines very unsatisfactory (which was no fault of the Pembroke shipwrights) but her performance was being adversely affected by using large quantities of insufficiently seasoned timber caused by the Admiralty's rush to use up stocks. Nicknamed the Queen's Bad Bargain, she was soon suffering from a rotting hull and within ten years was sold for scrap.

The Government eventually decided to reprieve the Pembroke and Sheerness yards and close only Deptford and Woolwich, making Pembroke the second royal dockyard, after Chatham, to be equipped for building iron ships.

'I suppose it's better than nothing,' commented John Berry.

'At least, dad, we've still got jobs,' countered Douglas. 'Not like those poor devils in Deptford and Woolwich.'

'I hear many of them are being transferred down here, so the navy must think there's going to be enough work for them as well as us,' said John.

John lapsed into moody silence. All these changes were hard to accept. In little more than a lifetime Pembroke shipbuilding had seen sail give way to steam and screw propellers replace paddlewheels. Now wood was being overtaken by iron and, eventually, steel. He hated the clamour, fumes and ugly foundries that were starting to infest the yard. The open slipways where timber was seasoned were being closed in under high roofs because iron, if left exposed to the elements, would soon rust. John was a craftsman who relished the scent of oak and pine and the gradual shaping of a length of timber beneath his plane or adze. He looked at Alfred.

'You're the new breed, son. You are going to have to learn new skills. You will be working with metal instead of wood. But it won't be the same. Iron doesn't speak to you like a piece of wood does.'

Alfred remembered these words as he confronted Annie. He understood what his father meant about the way a piece of wood could be moulded and shaped, but he also feared for his future if he didn't adapt to the rapid changes taking place around them. He was a young man with responsibilities: only two years married, he had a wife to provide for and already Annie had hinted she intended they would soon have other mouths to feed.

'We've got to look to the future,' he urged her. 'Everything's so uncertain here. Work is slowing up. The bosses are making changes but it's taking too long. There's work a-plenty up on the Clyde and the bosses are building homes for their workers.'

Annie could see his mind was made up and admitted to herself there was solid sense in much of what he said.

'OK,' she said, but without showing too much enthusiasm. 'If you think it's for the best, that's what we'll do. But promise me we'll come back if it doesn't work out or if things pick up here.'

Alfred willingly promised. It was what he had already decided they would do. He had as little desire as Annie to leave Pembroke and the family and was determined they would return at the first practical opportunity. But for now, he was sure the Clyde was the place to be.

The long move north was not as bad as Annie had imagined and turned out much as her husband had assured it would. There was security of work as the Glasgow shipyards went through an incredible period of expansion and prosperity. A scarcity of labour meant wages soared and the workers were able to negotiate improvements in conditions. The housing, too, had been far better than she had at first feared.

Clydeside was booming. What had previously been a relatively insignificant shipbuilding industry in the 1820s had expanded rapidly as wood and sail gave way to iron and steam. Engines devised by local man David Napier were installed in the boats that plied the Clyde estuary and across the Irish Sea. While Australia boomed from the rush to gold, it was a rush to iron that saw the townships along the Clyde expand like never before.

In 1830, Napier's cousin, James, invented a boiler that reduced fuel consumption by some thirty per cent. His cousin, Robert, moved down river from Lancefield to Govan at the end of the 1830s and rapidly secured some of the contracts for Cunard's transatlantic steamers. Men trained in the Napiers' yards formed new shipbuilding and marine-engine firms along the Clyde.

By 1864 there were more than twenty shipyards and by 1870 more than half the British shipbuilding workforce was based on the Clyde, producing half of Britain's tonnage of shipping. Shipyards had workforces of a thousand or more and, in 1861, were paying carpenters thirty shillings a week. Joiners were getting from twenty-two to twenty-six shillings depending on the quality of their work and in 1864 secured a rise of three shillings, while the carpenters' pay was increased to thirty-six shillings.

However, although 1865 opened with a whole year's work on hand, shipbuilding slackened off and carpenters suffered a pay cut of six shillings a week. Fortunately, another surge followed, and the late 1860s and first few years of the 1870s brought the century's biggest boom. Workers flooded in from all over Britain, including Alfred with wife Annie in tow, who was still nursing fears of miserable living conditions.

In a short span of time Govan changed from being a sleepy waterside rural waterside hamlet favoured by landscape artists to become the fifth largest burgh in Scotland, earning a description as 'the shipbuildingest burgh in the world'.

In 1793 only 224 families lived there. Most were handloom weavers or dyers occupying single-storey thatched cottages. In the surrounding countryside were several extensive and prosperous farms whose owners lived in nearby large country houses. The area's several market gardens and the fields on Govan Moor were famous for the quality of their potatoes, turnips and other crops. Thirty years later the local mines were producing enough coal to fill three hundred trading vessels a year. And with the coming of the shipyards the thatched cottages in the 'Auld Toon' and the country houses were demolished; in their place rose the first great blocks of sandstone tenements.

Soon there was hardly a soul crammed into the few square miles around Govan who did not depend on ships and shipbuilding. Housing was intolerably cramped and sub-standard. Big open spaces and grand city squares were being sold off for housing. Mansions that had housed a single family were converted into tenements housing a dozen or more. By the 1840s some of the city's housing conditions were regarded as among the worst in Europe. Lethal outbreaks of cholera, typhoid and typhus found easy and regular targets among the overcrowded and highly mobile population living in the foul 'backlands' and dingy lodging houses. Polluted water supplies, a smog-laden atmosphere and a lack of sunlight added to the inhabitants' health risks.

By 1864 the population had risen to 9000 and Govan gained the status of a burgh. The influx continued, and the 1891 census counted 61,500 residents within its boundaries. By 1912, there were 91,000 living there and all autonomy was lost.

Fortunately for Alfred and Annie, shipyard owner Alexander Stephen was one of the more enlightened entrepreneurs who tried to do something to ease these shocking conditions. In 1869, he bought the 18-acre Linthouse estate to the west of Govan to build his shipyard and converted the old mansion, one of Govan's most impressive country houses, to serve as offices and later (during World War I) as a canteen. The first ship was launched there in 1870 and the yard's engine and boiler works were completed the following year.

While overseeing the building of his shipyards, Alexander Stephen also ordered the construction of houses at nearby Linthouse for 120 men and their families. Alfred and Annie eventually moved there – into number 34 Linthouse Buildings – after initially finding rooms nearby at 19 Logie Street, a link between Landlands Road and Elder Street that is no longer there.

Boom times on the Clyde – a view of the Linthouse yards from Meadowside

If ever the much-abused expression 'a tight-knit community' was apt, it was here, among the tenement dwellers on the banks of the River Clyde in the late 1800s where almost everyone was a migrant enduring the daily struggles and challenges faced by newcomers the world over. Annie had often felt alone and far from home and this was the sort of communal support she craved and relied on, especially when she felt the first stirrings in her belly of the couple's first child.

'What wouldn't I give for some fresh air and a bit of peace and quiet,' she moaned to Alfred as lay alongside him and tried to shut out the noise rising up the stairwell.

She appreciated that Govan offered plenty of work and good wages but there was no relief from the noise, smoke and overcrowding as the town rapidly became home to heavy engineering plants, iron and steel manufacturing factories and to vast tidal and graving docks. It was a far cry from the life she and Alfred had left behind with the big skies of Pembrokeshire and its magnificent unspoilt coast so close to home.

Pembroke had its docks, slipways and workshops but nothing on a scale such as in Govan and in only a matter of minutes they could be among fields, headlands, hills and beaches along the Welsh coast where the air was fresh and clean ... and thankfully remains so today, preserved as a superb national park.

Annie did her best to accept the conditions in Linthouse but the odds were against her with the birth of Edwin Lloyd Berry on 11 March 1874. The poor mite died eight days later, suffering the agonies of stomatitis or, as Dr James Barras certified, derangement of the stomach.

Annie struggled on and by the end of the year was pregnant again and the couple was eventually cheered by the safe arrival of Alfred Berkeley, my great-grandfather, born at 10.50 pm on October 3, 1875. Where the

Berkeley comes from, no one knows. However, when Agness, Alfred's sister, gave birth in Milford a year later she also burdened her son, Thomas, with the Berkeley middle name. And it was extended into the next generation when Govan-born Alfred attached it to his son Wilfred, my father. Apart from these three instances it appears nowhere else on the many branches and twigs of the family tree.

As Annie strived to adapt to life in Govan she found her new role as a young mother helped her forge contacts and friendships among many of the other residents. Shared hardships and experiences brightened and eased the daily grind of tenement life. This was especially so when, well before Alfred Berkeley's second birthday, other women began noting her pallid look and regular bouts of sickness and asking if all was well. One of them gave her a friendly nudge.

'Looks as if there's another bairn on the way,' she commented with a smile.

'No doubt about it,' said another.

When they confirmed what Annie already suspected she happily broke the news to Alfred and at six o'clock on the morning of February 19, 1877, the couple welcomed the safe arrival of a boy they named Hugh.

It meant one more mouth to feed at a time when the shipyards began facing a precarious future. There was considerable industrial friction in the yard, culminating in a six-month strike by carpenters which, despite their persistence, ended with no increase in wages.

Alfred could see uncertain times ahead and began wondering whether their move so far from Milford had been such a good idea. It was a depressing thought and one he decided to keep to himself. Annie had enough to worry about ensuring their two boys stayed fed and healthy.

Down on the docks all the talk was of the competition the Glasgow yards were feeling from the ever-expanding Clydebank firms. Orders were declining and harder to win. There were fewer shifts available. With the introduction of steel hulls in the late 1870s, the shipbuilders needed to invest heavily in newer and more sophisticated equipment. That meant raising money, going into debt in a big way and cutting costs – and wages.

In 1874 the yard at Alexander Stephen was so busy that deliveries began to fall behind and several owners protested. Carpenters' wages were increased to eight pence an hour, but then, because of the increased costs, business began to decline. In April, one customer, the Hamburg Transatlantic Company, was obliged to ask for credit; although this was granted, the company was forced at the end of the year to relinquish one of the vessels under construction.

For many firms, however, their fate was decided not from within the industry but by the sudden and disastrous collapse in 1878 of the City of Glasgow Bank. The bank's operations had already been suspended in November and December the previous year when a deficit had been discovered of something like £500,000 in today's terms. An agreement with other Scottish banks and the closure of its New York office enabled it to resume trading to the extent that in June 1878 it declared a 12 per cent dividend and claimed to have 133 branches and deposits of around £600 million at today's prices.

It was what today we would call 'fake news'. Suddenly, on 2 October 1878, the directors announced the bank's closure. It was bankrupt. Behind a facade of profit and responsibility were nett liabilities of more than £500 million. These had been brought about by poorly secured loans and a broad portfolio of speculative investments in Australasian farming, foreign mining stocks and American railway shares. Balance sheets and profit and loss statements had been falsified and the share price held up by secret purchases of the bank's own stock. So successful was its deception that on its last business day the bank's £100 shares were selling at £236.

The shockwaves were widespread. Scores of Glasgow businesses failed because of the bank's collapse. Many shipbuilding firms were among them. In the subsequent general economic recession orders for ships slumped dramatically. It was little consolation that the directors were arrested, found guilty in Edinburgh High Court and sentenced to various terms of imprisonment.

Few were immune, but some were hit less hard than others. Shipbuilder Andrew Stephen, whose workers lived in Linthouse Buildings, was among the latter but it still meant tougher times for Alfred and Annie and the seed being sown of thoughts of a return to Pembroke. To help bolster their falling and uncertain income, Annie suggested taking in boarders.

'There's plenty of single men looking for somewhere to sleep,' she said.

Alfred greeted the idea with a puzzled look around their small flat.

'But where would they go?'

'We'll just have to squeeze up. The boys will have to sleep with us. We could do with the money and I'm sure it won't be for long.'

Alfred knew she was right – but was convinced her optimism was misplaced despite the boom or bust nature the shipbuilding industry had shown over the past century. The word down in the yard was that the boom times were well and truly over. Orders were scarce and it appeared that any recovery was going to be a long time coming. With such uncertainty, working hours varied considerably between the many shipyards. But although trade was somewhat slack, working hours on the Clyde were increased from 51 to 54 a week to give a faster turnaround on such work as did come in.

Annie put the word about and within next to no time welcomed two young single men as lodgers – cousins David Christie from Arbroath and William Christie from Methven, near Perth, engine fitters in the nearby yard.

Undeterred by the bank collapse, Alexander Stephen maintained its high reputation for reliability and first class vessels and obtained better prices than many of its competitors. As work was about to begin on laying down some vessels for its own account it received an order for four ships from a new company to be known as the Clan Line and agreed to take shares in the venture. Its first ship, the *Clan Alpine*, was built at Linthouse and launched at the end of 1878. And when the line later experienced some difficulty in arranging finance, builder Stephen arranged for extended terms to tide the young company over until more prosperous times.

By the end of the year, great-great-grandfather Alfred Berry's gloomy prediction was beginning to fade. Business had revived and Alexander Stephen had recorded the second highest output for the year among Clyde shipbuilders. The residents of Linthouse Buildings celebrated long and hard when they took their short break for the New Year holiday.

'I reckon we've earned this and more,' said Alfred as he shared a jug of ale brought from the pub by his young lodgers.

He got no argument from them, but the bosses were more forthcoming. They claimed the men had worked much harder than usual in the week before Hogmanay to boost their pay packets. One voiced the opinion that 'If workmen would work all the year round as they did this week it would make a great deal of difference, to themselves and to the yard'.

He probably had a point because although the yard entered 1880 with so many orders that it stopped tendering for new vessels, work did not advance as rapidly as might have been expected. Workers were becoming less compliant; stoppages and strikes were more frequent and productivity was not always as expected.

Alfred sensed the change in mood and remained anxious about the future. This was not helped by the cramped conditions at home and the lack of clean air and open spaces for Annie and their boys. Their only escape was to Elder Park, just around the corner from the tenements and still a treasured and well cared for oasis between docks and tenements, but it was hardly what he considered an open space compared to the wild Pembrokeshire coast.

Elder Park on the left and the terrace where the Linthouse Buildings, home of the Berry family, once stood

One slight consolation was that Linthouse considered itself separate from Govan and a cut above its neighbouring settlement. Former residents remember it as the place of the 3 Ps – no pubs, no picture houses and no pawnshops. Shops or other commercial premises occupied the bottom floors of the four-storey tenements. There were two or three flats on each floor and a single toilet on the half landing shared by each floor. The homes mostly consisted of three rooms, although some had only two. The entire 'close' shared one washhouse and used a drying green at the rear of the building.

Annie was feeling the strain and often wondered about Alfred's promise that they would return to Pembroke if things didn't work out. She welcomed the extra money from her lodgers but was increasingly depressed by the irksome lack of living space. And once again there were stirrings from within her body as another child began to make its presence felt. She broke the news to Alfred and made her feelings known.

'I'd like to go home,' she said. 'You promised we would and this is no place to bring up children.'

He readily agreed and admitted he shared her longing to be back with their families in Pembroke.

'Perhaps you should write and let your folks know the news about the babe,' he suggested and wrapped an arm around her. He gave her a smile. 'And while you're at it maybe find out if there's work to be had for a shipwright who's worked on the Clyde.'

The relief was palpable. Their hidden thoughts and concerns were out in the open and there was little dispute about their plans, even when Alfred suggested they delay their return to Wales until after the birth and to wait past winter when travelling with three young children would be easier.

Any joy at the thought of returning home rapidly evaporated with the birth of their third son in Linthouse Buildings on 25 February 1879. Following the custom of the times, he was named Edwin Lloyd Berry in memory of his earlier sibling. Tragically he carried the ill-starred name a mere four months before succumbing to a three-day bout of meningitis on 2 July 1879. Anne was plunged back into the doldrums she had valiantly fought against and pleaded with Alfred to return to Milford. But he was reluctant to leave.

He argued that things were looking up. The Alexander Stephen shipyard had begun the year with 31,000 tonnes of work on hand (rising in a few months to 40,000 tonnes) and a carpenter's wage was increased to 31s 6d a week (equivalent to about £90, or £4680 a year, in today's purchasing power).

'It's good money,' he reasoned. 'You need to recover, get strong again. Let's see out this year, then we'll go.'

That may have been the plan, but a lack of planning in other directions (and maybe the excesses of year-end festivities) worked against them once more and early in 1880 Annie was carrying another child. Fortunately, the birth on 30 October 1880 of their only daughter, Elizabeth, was trouble free and this time Annie at last had her way.

She and Alfred and the three only Scottish-born members of the Berry family returned to Wales, to the family home in Military Road, Pennar, in time for the birth of Sidney in September 1882. He was followed only twelve months later in September 1883 by the son doomed in a desperate third time lucky attempt to be given the name Edwin but who eventually fared little better than his earlier siblings; he was killed in action on Flanders Fields in 1917.

It was one of this Scottish 'clan' – my grandfather, Alfred Berkeley – who later took the brave step of crossing the border into England to find work in the dockyards in Chatham. His brothers also made similar moves to Devonport, Portsmouth, London and Coventry. And so began the English branch of a tree that for centuries had been deeply rooted in the soil of Wales.

Today there are merely seven Berrys listed in the Pembrokeshire phone book. Military Road, however, remains much as it would have appeared when this was the family home – a long undulating street of neat and well-kept terraced homes leading out to a headland overlooking the sea and with views down the hillside to the docks and shipyard. Windows and doors have been modernised, the inevitable satellite dishes adorn the roofs and walls, and backyard and attic extensions have been subtly added. But the essential character remains of a solid working class street with solid working class values.

Little wonder that when great-grandfather Alfred Jabez Berry died suddenly here on March 22, 1929, at the age of 80, the *West Wales Guardian* recorded the death of 'one of Pembroke Dock's oldest and most respected inhabitants'. It reported his funeral at Llanion Cemetery was attended by 'a large gathering of sympathisers, including many of the deceased's former dockyard colleagues'.

The newspaper noted that Alfred was 'a regular attendant and devoted member' of the Pennar Wesleyan Church, of which he had been a trustee for many years.

His will granted probate and 'all my real and personal property' to his youngest son,

58 Military Road, Pembroke Dock, the longtime family home to Alfred Jabez and Annie

my grand-uncle Wilfred, and listed effects totalling £56 – roughly equivalent to a year's basic wage.

After the addition of Norman in December 1887 and Wilfred in December 1890, the family settled down in their Military Road terraced cottage, to spend the rest of their days in working class comfort as solid and respected members of the local community. Welsh-born, Scots-born all together, and with Alfred Jabez's sister, Agness, soon to graft a Cornish branch on to the family tree the Berrys had forged their own Celtic Triple Crown.

DEATH IN THE DOCKYARD

EARLY ON A JULY morning in 1883, Alfred Berry and heavily pregnant wife Annie, weeks away from giving birth to Edwin, sat in their kitchen table at 58 Military Road, Pennar, staring grim-faced at the newspaper spread out on the table before them. The big, bold headlines were frightening; the long columns of news below them even more so. The terse confronting words across the top of the page said it all - *Shipyard Disaster on Scotland's River Clyde*. A hundred and twenty-three dead. Many more maimed and injured.

'That's our shipyard,' said Alfred, staring at the newspaper headlines, his voice a tremulous mix of fear and anxiety. 'We could have been there.'

His finger traced down the list of the dead. So many familiar names.

'That could have been me,' he whispered.

Annie put a consoling hand on top of his. Even from this safe distance in terms of miles and time it seemed like a narrow escape. The news brought home the ever-present danger the dockyard workers faced in those days long before the words 'workplace' and 'safety' had been paired and voiced as one.

Annie leaned forward, looking over her husband's shoulder. as he read the roll call of the dead. The address of some of those killed – Linthouse Buildings – leapt out at them early in the list. There was a gasp from Annie.

'Oh, look, there's that young man from number 30, almost next door,' she said.

Her finger hovered over the name Daniel McKay, an apprentice fitter aged eighteen.

'And there's another,' she said, pointing to Angus McNab, a trainee engineer from number fourteen.

Further down were the names of more men Alfred had worked with or passed on the stairs on their way to and from work. There was William

Duncan, a carpenter, from number thirty and James Hall, a joiner from number eighteen.

Others from Linthouse Buildings to lose their lives were labourer James Carbary, age 22, apprentice fitter James Hutchison, 17, and labourer Peter Bradley, 32.

The list went on and on, a litany of tragedy that Alfred and Annie knew could well have included Alfred's name. One victim's body remained unclaimed. The paper recorded that 'upon this body there were found a caulk-line, a gimlet, a two-foot rule, a pocket knife marked W.H., a pair of boot laces in pocket, three lead pencils etc.'

'Poor man,' said Annie. 'To die like that and then have no one to claim you or to bury you.'

They continued reading in gloomy silence.

More than two hundred miles away, word had spread quicker than the echo of a riveter's hammer in the Govan dry dock. The tenements of the Linthouse Buildings resounded to frantic shouts and the pounding of boots on the stairs as the bringers of tragic news knocked on doors and yelled the sparse details.

'A ship's gone down,' was the terse message.

They needed to say little more. The wives, mothers and children who rushed to their doors and gathered in the stairwells on Tuesday July 3, 1883 knew what it meant. They didn't require lengthy explanations; the urgency and brevity of the messengers' cries said it all. The commotion voiced their worst fears; the dread they lived with every day as their men-folk trudged off for another shift in the Glasgow shipyards.

Already there was a hurrying stream of people flowing towards the massive steel gates of the fortress-like premises of Alexander Stephen and Sons. They were stumbling and pushing, showing little regard for those around them despite their common panic. Everyone in that river of desperate people was focused on the fate of someone they cared about who was working behind those formidable high red brick walls.

Ahead, sirens wailed. Burly, official-looking men in black suits and bowler hats stood at the shipyard gates, trying to hold back the growing crush of people. Emergency carriages threaded their way in from the street, the horses steaming and twitchy, their drivers yelling to clear a path through the crowd.

A voice called out 'It's the *Daphne*'. Others took up the refrain. Cries of 'Oh my God' or simply someone's name greeted the news. The fears of those who knew that was where their menfolk were working soared even higher. Others hugged themselves in silent relief at their good fortune or let out a gentle sigh at they drew their children closer, comforted by knowing their man was working on some other ship.

Of the two hundred workers on board the 460-tonne *Daphne* as she flipped over, one hundred and twenty-three had died. At first, it had seemed like any of the hundreds of launches that took place up and down the Clyde. But because her owner, the Laird Line of Glasgow, was eager to have her finished for the Glasgow Fair holidays the *Daphne* had an unusually large number of workmen on board. Her engines were also placed on board before the launch, and her boilers were to have been installed immediately afterwards.

Shipbuilders worked largely by rule of thumb and experience; they therefore had little knowledge of how to calculate the stability of their vessels. There were the usual two anchors and cables in place to steady the vessel after she entered the water. But this checking apparatus failed to function. The starboard anchor moved some six or seven yards, but the port anchor dragged for about sixty yards.

The *Daphne* floated perfectly for less than three minutes before the river's current caught her at a critical moment and turned her on to her port side. She rolled over and sank.

Most of the men on board were trapped inside the holds, engine-rooms and cabins where they had been working. As the ship toppled over, others were tumbled into the water.

Men and boys who had been putting the finishing touches were suddenly shrieking and yelling. Twenty or so managed to scramble on to the vessel's hull or clung on to its side. Instead of the cheers and hurrahs normal on such occasions, the air was filled with the screams of drowning men. A flotilla of small boats that had been assisting at the launch rushed to the scene, gathering up the desperate survivors. Although divers were sent down immediately, they could do little to help. It was only days later that the *Daphne* was partially moved, and almost three weeks before she was docked.

One survivor, a joiner named Kinnaird, was reported as saying that before the accident there were so many men and boys on deck that it was difficult to move.

'I cannot possibly describe the heartbreaking scenes I witnessed,' he added.

'It must have been terrible,' said Annie. 'To think that …'

She let her words hang in the air, her thoughts needing no further expansion. It was little more than a year since they had returned from Scotland and the lengthy report stirred so many memories. The move to Clydeside had not been as bad as she had first feared and she and Alfred had not only returned home to more prosperous times in the Pembroke dockyard but, to the delight of their parents, had also brought their three children born on Scottish soil – one of them my paternal grandfather, Alfred Berkeley Berry.

These provide my direct links to a third Celtic nation.

NOTE: At an enquiry into the sinking of the *Daphne* the yard owners were exonerated from any blame, leading to claims of a cover up. One outcome was to limit personnel aboard to only those necessary to moor the ship after the launch. The ship was raised and repaired at Govan Dry Docks and emerged as the *Rose*.

Such was the scale and tragedy of the disaster that there are two SS *Daphne* memorials in Glasgow. One is in Elder Park, Govan, opposite where the Berrys once lived, and the other on the other side of the Clyde in Victoria Park, Whiteinch, representing the loss to those communities involved.

WORKHOUSE WOES

As I sit at my desk in my comfortable all-mod-cons apartment and trawl back through the years it is humbling to discover that only two or three generations ago there were forebears on both sides of my ancestral line who endured lengthy periods living in workhouses. With no social services to turn to, they were entirely dependent upon the charity of local communities for all their basic needs. They were homeless and destitute.

Some were even born in these grim Victorian institutions; several died there. The children often knew no other existence until they were deemed old enough to be turned out into the world to fend for themselves. For all of them, the workhouse was their last port of call in their battle to survive, and the only means parents had of providing even the most meagre food for their children.

Not one of them, as best as I can tell, was what today would be labelled a bludger, a dole cheat or a rorter of the system. Most were honest toilers. They worked long hours in the most menial of jobs that were usually repetitive, tedious, dirty and dangerous. Conditions were primitive and harsh and there were few safety regulations. Wages were never more than subsistence level yet had to support the large families that were common in a society that knew next to nothing about birth control. Lack of education – many of my ancestors were illiterate – ensured there was scant chance of ever improving their lot in life.

In total contrast, and little more than a century later, although my lifestyle in the middle-income bracket is classified as merely modest after being a so-called 'wage slave' all my working life, I am well clothed and amply fed and able to indulge in my chosen pleasures of food, travel, theatre and music without fear of penury into the foreseeable future as I flit between apartments I own at opposite ends of the world. There is much to be thankful for and so little cause for discontent when this existence is compared to the daily routine suffered by my ancestors scarcely a hundred years ago.

Whether the shelter was provided by the local Poor Law Union, the workhouse or an 'industrial school' the conditions and the regulations imposed on my pauper relatives were depressingly similar. But when times got tough, with no roof over your head and several young mouths to feed, the workhouse was the only place to go. Here at least there was a bed of sorts, gruel and bread for sustenance and sometimes even a rudimentary education that offered some prospect of eventual employment.

Maybe the breadwinner had died – industrial accidents were rife - or deserted their family. Sometimes it was the mother who had died and the father could not juggle work and childcare. Some were committed to the workhouse, others went voluntarily, checking in and out as their meagre fortunes fluctuated. It was a life of endless poverty, sickness and threadbare clothes that continues to shock with each new discovery of an ancestor listed as an inmate of one of these grim institutions. Gazing out from my comfortable middle class cocoon it is salutary to be reminded that it is from several of these survivors, sometimes listed as 'pauper', that my family is descended.

Their institutional surroundings were uniformly grim. Workhouse superintendents were invariably unfeeling martinets. Some were even fraudsters and lawbreakers guilty of crimes worse than those committed by the people in their care. They were allocated minimal resources and were beholden to committees of management dominated by smug do-gooders who saw poverty as a social crime. Pity and understanding were in short supply; punishment, chastisement and penalties were plentiful.

Several individuals and whole families on both my parental lines experienced life in one of these forbidding establishments. Many on the maternal side struggled to eke out a living at the lowest down-trodden levels of the workforce and at various times were forced to call upon this miserly public purse for shelter and sustenance for themselves and their children.

Even the more prosperous paternal side, where the breadwinners were predominantly journeymen with employable skills, did not escape the stigma of the workhouse. Misfortune and penury blighted family members as recently as the early twentieth century when my great-grandparents were beginning our ascension into middle class respectability.

One of the best documented examples of this endless struggle against the odds was found when tracing the life of great-great-uncle George Waymouth Berry, born in that 'lost' village of Coombs in 1851, the youngest son of John and Ann Berry.

Beyond the mystery of why he was named Waymouth, there was little to question about much of his life. Like so many of his family, he found steady and skilled employment as a carpenter and shipwright, moving back and forth to wherever work was available in the nation's Admiralty shipyards – Pembroke, Chatham (living only a mile or so from where I was born), Portsmouth and finally back in Pembroke.

And there, in his early fifties, he simply disappears. He becomes my man of mystery. There are records of his early life, his marriage to Mary Ann Green, the births (and deaths) of their eight children and, throughout the 1890s, the days of destitution of Mary and several of their children as they depend for food and shelter on the resources of the Haverfordwest Workhouse.

George is briefly mentioned in workhouse records as an absentee bread-winner and also as the 'father' when youngest daughter Florence Sophia was born on 8 January 1897. And when Mary dies on 16 February 1910 she is recorded as 'wife of George Berry shipwright and journeyman'.

But little more than a year later, when daughter Ada marries John James in Haverfordwest on 22 August 1911, he is recorded as 'deceased'.

All manner of resources have been enlisted in my search for George in his latter years. But to no avail. There is a George Berry – or even more than one of that name - being fined or imprisoned for several minor crimes around the Haverfordwest area over succeeding years but none bear that unique identifier of a middle name Waymouth.

If he emigrated or went to sea, he left no trace. And to do so would seem at odds with the way he stayed close to Mary and their children throughout what were often extremely turbulent and trying times. But he was nowhere to be seen when things hit rock bottom and Mary Anne Berry stood before the Haverfordwest Poor Law Union's receiving officer Joseph John, on Monday, 25 July 1890.

Her life had reached its lowest ebb. As she explained to Mr John, she and her six children, who stood meekly at her side, were destitute.

'We have nothing, sir,' she said. 'I cannot feed them. No one will take us in.'

Mr John considered the forlorn faces before him – four boys and two girls, the oldest a scrawny lad of twelve and the youngest a babe in arms, newly born and still at her mother's breast. He noted the desperation on the woman's face and the way the children gathered close to her. Their clothes were ragged and old yet there was about them a neatness and an attempt at cleanliness. He also detected pride and determination beneath the despair; this was a mother who cared.

However, he had his duty to perform; there were questions that had to be asked before incurring costs to the parish.

'And where is Mr Berry, your husband?'

'I wish I knew, sir,' whispered Mary in her broad Cockney accent, wondering how she had ever fallen for the bright

The former Haverfordwest workhouse
[copyright Haverfordwest Civic Society]

young Welshman who had breezed into her life twenty years ago and whisked her away from family and friends.

'He can't earn enough to support us,' she added.

The hopes and promises of their early days together in Shoreditch had soon faded as George moved from job to job, and from town to town, while keeping her in an almost permanent state of pregnancy with seven kids in 14 years and their first-born dying when only five years old.

As mentioned, this youngest brother of my great-grandfather Alfred Jabez Berry had started out all right in a solid Welsh working class home, doing as his brothers and father had done before him and learning the trade of joiner and shipwright. But while Alfred progressed steadily through life with gainful employment, marriage to a local girl and eventual recognition as a pillar of the local community, George had other ideas. He decided the grass was greener, and more lucrative, far from solid family life in the Berrys' house in Marine Gardens, Milford, with its view out over the Haven and the expanding dockyard on the facing shore at Pembroke. After all, as his father and brothers kept hammering into him, a man with a trade would never be short of work. A man who could shape a piece of wood was sure to find gainful employment, even if it meant forsaking life close to the water. It was a trade that could be applied almost anywhere and especially in the big cities upcountry where, George reasoned, better money was surely to be made than he would ever earn in Pembroke Dock.

So he headed for London, the River Thames and the shipyards around Woolwich and Greenwich. He reckoned there would be no problem finding temporary lodgings as his elder brother, Joseph, now lived here in Queen Street with wife Sophie after bucking the family tradition and opting for life as a grocer.

It was here that George's path crossed that of Mary Anne Green, a true Cockney and a domestic servant in the home of John Hart, a baker running a booming business in the bustling heart of Hackney at 167 Hoxton Street. While George made good-hearted fun of Mary's Cockney whine, she quickly fell for his lilting Welsh brogue and devil-may-care ways.

When George found work harder to come by than he had ever dreamed would be the case, Mary yielded to his plea to return with him to Wales, where he believed his family's contacts would surely help him find a job and – this was the icing on the cake for Mary – they could get married.

As she stood defeated and patiently waited for Mr John to decide her fate, Mary thought ruefully back to that day on 17 March 1875 when she and George said their vows in Steynton Parish Church in front of the vicar, the Rev M B Thomas. But there was little point in dwelling on the past. Regrets were futile. There was no turning back the clock. She knew marrying George had been the biggest mistake of her young life. From then on, everything went downhill.

When George's hopes of work in Pembroke Dock came to nothing he decided they should move all the way back across the country to the Admiralty dockyard at Chatham, in Kent, which at least was closer to Mary's old home in London's East End. They obtained lodgings at 8 Woodland Terrace, Gillingham – coincidentally a short walk from where my grandfather and George's nephew, Alfred Berkeley Berry, would settle half a century later – in time for Mary to give birth on 18 September 1876 to a daughter they grandly named Adelaide Lavinia. Within months Mary was pregnant again and in July 1878 the couple welcomed their first son, John Edwin.

From then on Mary felt her life was spinning out of control. In his endless pursuit of work, George dictated a move back to Milford.

'But why, George, why?' pleaded Mary, now pregnant yet again, with second son William James who was born in July 1880.

'It's the job,' replied George. 'We go where the Admiralty tells us to. There's nothing I can do about it.'

Mary suspected there was more to it than that. She sometimes wondered if the fault lay more with George than with the Admiralty. Other men seemed to settle into the yard's workforce without continually uprooting their family in the search for jobs. His own father and brothers were solid proof of that.

She had scarcely recovered from giving birth to William than they were packing up their meagre belongings yet again. George, ever optimistic, assured her it was all for the best; a good move.

'Where to this time?' asked a weary Mary.

'Portsea Island,' was George's gruff reply.

Mary had never heard of it and pressed him for more information.

'It's the place to be,' he tried to assure her. 'It's on the south coast in Hampshire, Britain's biggest island, right on the shores of the Solent and the English Channel. Plenty of good sea air for you and the kids.'

Almost as an aside he added that it was at the heart of the massive naval base at Portsmouth, one time home of Nelson's fleet that fought the Spanish Armada and where the admiral's flagship, the *Victory*, now rested. It was in the dockyard here that he expected to find work.

One thing George did not mention was that although the booming city was blessed in part by streetlights, piped water and mains sewers, much of Portsea's housing was squalid and badly built with damp dilapidated cellars. Despite a burgeoning middle class in its outer suburbs, this was still a rough and ready naval town where crime was a regular part of daily life and the under-policed streets were rife with drunks, prostitutes, pickpockets, vagrants and beggars.

The local death rate of children under five was well above the national average, caused by malnutrition and lack of clothing, a statistic that might have caused Mary to have second thoughts. At first they settled into 6

Wingfield St, Portsea. Lavinia died, age 5, when the family were living at No.152

Unicorn Street, Portsea, in the dirtiest, most overcrowded part of town, bordering the high forbidding walls of the naval dockyard.

Within a year they had moved to equally depressing accommodation at nearby Wingfield Street where the eldest of her growing brood, Adelaide Lavinia, died at the age of five from a combination of measles and bronchitis – and Mary was pregnant yet again.

Within months of Adelaide's death on 20 March 20, 1882, she gave birth, in 1883, to Lillian Elizabeth and became ever more fearful for the welfare of herself and her family in Wingfield Street's squalid surroundings. Outbreaks of cholera and other epidemics were frequent and the house was damp and cold. Few of the small terraced houses where George and Mary lived exist today, although there is a small enclave of grander dwellings on its fringes that ironically includes the beautifully preserved grand Regency house where the chronicler of the poor and oppressed, Charles Dickens, was born. Maybe it was here, with such squalor almost on his doorstep, that he was first inspired to document so vividly the living conditions of Britain's underclass. The maze of narrow streets of Mary's time still exist and, sadly, still exude an air of hopelessness and poverty from the modern council-built tenements that replace the slums of a century ago.

Mary pleaded frequently with George for them to return to Milford where the air was cleaner and there was little of Portsea's slum-like overcrowding.

'It's not so much for me, but at least think of the children,' she urged.

Her pleading failed to move him; he seemed deaf to her demands. He had become stubborn and morose. Too often he came home with the heavy smell of beer on his breath and scant money left from his wages to pay for their food. It was as if the responsibilities of being a wage-earner and father were all too much. Yet that did not stop him demanding his conjugal rights and once again Mary found herself pregnant. It was the final straw.

'I'm not going to bury another child here,' she snapped at him. 'You'll take us back to Milford or me and the kids will make our own way there.'

Living conditions in Robert Street, Milford's busy commercial hub one block back from the cliff top harbour front, were little better. Mary, with five children under 10 and a husband who lacked the drive and commitment she noted in the rest of the Berry clan, was burdened with drudgery and worry. She was grateful for what money George so grudgingly gave and reluctantly tolerated his surly insistent presence to the extent that even though it had become a loveless marriage she again found herself pregnant within a year of Ada's birth.

This was the final straw. Less than six months after delivering Albert Edward from her womb, Mary threw herself and her children on the mercy of the guardians of the grim Haverfordwest Poor Law Union workhouse.

As she watched Joseph John's pen inscribe her details on to the forms in front of him, she thought again about her response. Did she really wish she knew where George had gone; did she even care? All she was concerned about was caring for her family and George could take care of himself.

'I don't really know where he is, sir,' she said. 'He's gone and left us with nothing. Last I heard he was boarding with a widow lady up by Robert Street, in Manchester Square.'

The receiving officer's face remained impassive. Every day he heard stories of neglect, desertion, sickness and abject poverty and of families who could not put food on the table, fuel on the fire or shoes on their children's feet. He could not afford to display emotion or appear to favour one unfortunate over another, even though he knew some were more deserving than others; that there were those who made no attempt to improve themselves and others to whom the workhouse was a refuge of last resort and were almost too proud to depend on its charity.

Mr John sensed the woman standing before him was firmly in the latter category. She had been reduced to shedding the remnants of her pride and was here out of desperation for the welfare of her children. He signed the forms with a flourish.

'You will be admitted and placed in the care of Mr Thomas,' he said. 'You will be a charge against the parish and your first meals will be supper.'

Mary took a long deep breath of relief. Her shoulders drooped as the tension ebbed. This was not where she wanted to be, but it meant the children would be fed and have a roof over their heads.

'Thank you, sir,' she said. 'I am truly grateful.'

Mary and the children filed slowly through the entrance door into the main workhouse block to be met by the institution's master, John Thomas, and the matron, Martha Martin. Mr Thomas, a sombre-looking 51-year-old, had somewhat unusually been allowed to continue as master despite the recent death of his wife, Annie, who had previously served as the workhouse matron.

Rather than follow the usual procedure and seek a married couple following Annie Thomas's death, the guardians had appointed Martha

Martin, the 30-year-old daughter of the assistant overseer at the nearby St Thomas Green Infirmary to take her place, although John Thomas continued to hope that his eldest daughter, Maud, would eventually return from her training as a nurse at the vast and highly praised Crumpsall workhouse in Manchester with its infirmary and specialist wards and room for 1600 inmates.

John Thomas nodded a greeting at Mary and conducted a hurried roll call, checking her name and those of the children against a large register spread out on a table in front of him. He folded the book shut, his duties done.

'I'll leave you with matron,' he said. 'Wait here and the doctor will be with you soon.'

There would be no admission into the grim rooms beyond until they had undergone the inevitable medical examination for lice, vermin and signs of disease or open sores. The children's hair was cropped right back. Then came the humiliating experience of being stripped, bathed and issued with a workhouse uniform. Their clothes were taken away to be washed, disinfected and stored until they were ready to return to the outside world. Finally came the worst moment of all – the heart wrenching separation as the children were removed from Mary's close attention and the boys were divided from the girls.

Mary held on tight to baby Albert and kept her face averted to hide her tears as she wrapped her free arm in a tight hug around each of the other children in turn.

'We'll be together soon,' she whispered in a brave attempt at reassurance as a young female assistant summoned led them off to their separate wards in different blocks of the workhouse.

It was an optimistic but forlorn promise. For the next four years, Mary and her children spent much of their lives in the small, dirty, poorly ventilated and badly heated wards enclosed by the thick stone walls of this gaunt institution. On several occasions she obtained permission to leave but inevitably she returned, sometimes merely for an overnight stay – in before supper and out after breakfast – and on other occasions to spend time with her children. Always her conduct was recorded as 'good' and her prime concern was the welfare of her children.

Years of deprivation, sub-standard housing and poor nutrition had, however, taken their toll. Much more so than was indicated by the single annotation that she was 'unwell' when she asked to be taken in for an overnight stay on Thursday 20 August 20. With year-old Albert in her arms she sought a bed and a meal. She stayed for supper – a greasy wooden bowl of weak gruel – and breakfast, which was much the same but with the addition of a chunk of bread.

She struggled on and began the new year by securing 12-year-old son John's discharge so that he could stay with his uncle in London. But her own health was getting no better in the cold Welsh winter and on Saturday 23 April she was discharged by the workhouse to go into the Haverfordwest Infirmary for an unspecified operation. Several weeks later, on Thursday 22 June, she and son John reappeared before receiving officer Joseph John seeking readmission to the workhouse. John had been sent back from his uncle in London as 'unwell' and Mary was returning from the infirmary.

And so she battled on, seeking escape from the confines of the workhouse yet drawn back time and again to spend even a few moments with her children. Always her conduct was 'good' and she seemed to come and go almost at will despite the seemingly rigid conditions laid down by the Poor Law Act and by the local guardians.

Through it all there was never a mention or a record of husband George. On Thursday 9 August 1892, Mary asked to be readmitted to the workhouse. Her reason was basic and enough to touch the hardest heart.

'I can't bear to be parted from my sons,' she told the receiving officer.

She was given dinner and supper and left the next day after breakfast, taking sons John, now a hardened lad of 14, and William, 12, with her.

Sadly, no matter how much Mary tried, life on the outside could not be sustained and the family continued to rely on the workhouse for their food and lodgings. Her frail and sick body didn't help and she was sent from the workhouse to the infirmary on Tuesday 2 May 1893, for an operation on her face. A week later she was back with her children in the workhouse.

They remained there throughout the summer, although Mary would make occasional forays out into the town, keeping in touch with her few friends and alert for any news of her wayward husband. It was a sporadic and low-key version of what today would be labelled as networking – a finger on the weak pulse of opportunities, a street-wise eye open for any avenue of survival.

It meant she was again able to offer a special reason when pleading for a discharge from the workhouse on Monday 2 October. There was a gleam of pride in her eyes as she put her case.

'I want to take my son John,' she explained. 'He has work. I am putting him to service as an errand boy.'

For John it meant the end of more than three years of sleeping on a chaff mattress laid on three wooden planks on an iron bedstead; of subsisting on monotonous meals of gruels, stews and bread; of being confined for exercise and fresh air to the courtyards between the accommodation blocks; of being cold in winter and almost suffocated in summer. Whatever employment, whatever master he was going to, would be better than this.

Soon, however, he decided a precarious existence pedalling around the streets of Haverfordwest as an errand boy was not for him. He enlisted in the Royal Navy as a boy second class and went on to serve right through the Great War on HMS *Berwick* until being demobbed on 18 November 1919 with the lowly rank of able-bodied seaman. He was awarded the Naval Medal, the Victory Star, a war gratuity and a naval pension. He eventually died of phthisis or tuberculosis of the lungs in Pontardwe, Glamorgan, in November 1934.

John may have been off her hands, but Mary still had five other children in the workhouse to fret over. Their welfare was also her prime concern and on Saturday 4 November 1893, she asked permission to take 11-year-old Lillian away to Milford for a week.

'It's for the good of her health,' Mary told the officer considering her application. 'A bit of sea air and she has cousins there.'

She made no mention that it was also in Milford – in Manchester Square halfway along Robert Street where the cousins lived – that husband George had last been living. On the night of the 1891 census he was listed as a shipwright boarding in the house of widow Albina Phillips and her son in Manchester Square, Steynton – now Milford Haven.

The request was granted, as workhouse manager John Thomas duly noted in the register of admissions and discharges. Almost a month later, on Thursday, 30 November, he recorded Lillian's return and that she was to receive the special Class 7 children's diet. This included slightly more meat and perhaps some milk or tea in addition to the staples of vegetable broth and bread served to the adults in greater measure, although it was hardly a sufficient barrier to the bone-chilling Welsh winter.

Branded as paupers and sustained by the workhouse, the family struggled on through Christmas and into the new year. The one absentee, William, who had been on the outside for almost eighteen months, working in the grocery shop of his cousin Dundas Berry in Woolwich, was – in the terse words of Mr Thomas's register – 'returned to his mother' on 22 February 1894. London was not for him: the 14-year-old was destitute and hungry. The workhouse had become the only 'home' he knew.

Mary, however, remained undaunted. She was determined there would be a better life for her children. On May 30 she was allowed to take Ada out of the workhouse 'to go to Mr Lewis' where the 10-year-old set out on the trail taken by so many working class girls, her mother included, and went 'into service' as a domestic servant.

Mary returned to the workhouse with Lillian and Albert on Monday 27 August. They had dinner and supper and left after breakfast the next day – the last time there is any record of them in the Haverfordwest Poor Law Union's workhouse register.

It therefore came as a major surprise to see when, on 8 January 1897 and at the age of 43, Mary gives birth to Florence Sophia it is George, described as a shipwright journeyman, whose name appears on the birth certificate as the girl's father.

Mary was then was living in Grove Row, Haverfordwest, a laneway close to the Oak Inn on St Thomas Green. This raises more questions than it answers. Where had George been since the last mention of him on the 1891 census and all the time his wife and kids were living in the workhouse?

Why was he living in relative comfort as a boarder while they were confined within the grim walls of an institution? The most charitable answer is

College Green Haverfordwest where Mary Berry and her family lived after leaving the workhouse

that although he could not earn enough to pay for rent and food for the entire family, he could scrape by as an allegedly single man. As a journeyman (one who is paid by the day, or a casual in present terminology) he would have good days and bad days and sometimes have a run of employment enough to feed himself and Mary and maybe one or more of the children – which could explain her random comings and goings at the workhouse.

By the time of the 1901 census Mary's workhouse days and life as a pauper appeared to be behind her. She was again living in St Thomas Green, listed as married but with no sign of husband George. Four of her children – Ada, Albert, Joseph and Florence – were still with her. William was working for his grocer uncle, Dundas Berry, in Samuel Street, Woolwich; John was in the Royal Navy and there is no record of what Lily was doing at that time.

By 1911 Ada had met and married, on 22 August, John James from Haverfordwest, a signalman with the Great Western Railway. She died in Haverfordwest in 1963 at the age of 78. Lily reappeared in 1912 when she apparently married William James, quite possibly the brother of Ada's husband, in Haverfordwest.

Joseph, who found work as a boot and shoe salesman, hardly reached adulthood. He died from a dilated heart in the Haverfordwest Infirmary on 30 April 1908, at the age of 20. Mary, her body frail from years of childbirth, malnutrition, impoverishment and endless stress, died from heart disease on 16 February 1910, with son William at her side. But at least she had the consolation of knowing none of her surviving children, nor were any of their offspring, likely to again be labelled as impoverished and destitute paupers.

Despite trawling through every possible resource, the elusive George remains a mystery that I still hope to resolve. He was not present at the death of either wife Mary or their son Joseph and when Ada married John James in 1912 he was recorded as deceased. He may have gone to sea, as many shipwrights did, or even sought a new life overseas. But there are no records to support such theories and the fact that Ada knew of his death suggests he remained in the Milford area and kept well away from his family as well as staying well clear of any form of officialdom – even to the extent of leaving no record of his death.

Other researchers who have helped in my bid to track him down have suggested he emigrated or went to sea, where he could use his skills as a ship's carpenter. But he appears on no shipping records, passenger lists or immigration files.

There are no clues as to how or why he was given the unusual second name of Waymouth. Maybe he was conceived in the resort of that name during a holiday excursion by his parents, William and Ann. It gives him the defining sort of tag that is usually so useful when trawling through lists and records and trying to separate one George from another. Yet the only other of that name so far found in numerous global searches was married in Sydney in 1912 and proved to have no connection whatsoever with my Milford Haven George.

He remains my mysterious disappearing great-great-uncle, but the search goes on.

THE COUSINS FROM
CYBERSPACE

HAD IT NOT BEEN for a couple of those delightful out-of-the-blue moments that make family history so endlessly exciting, lighthouse-keeper Charles Edwin Nicholas would probably have never pointed me in the direction of a Cornish heritage. He would have remained perched on an outlying branch of my family tree, unacknowledged and unexplored.

These eventually life-changing events initially occurred in the form of two emails from among the several received over time from total strangers in Hampshire, Essex, Swindon, Wales, Cornwall, California and elsewhere, as well as close to the maternal grandparental home in Yorkshire.

Both were from people advancing positive proof that they and I enjoyed some close family relationship.

The links between us – and their reason for contacting me – were to be found on our various family trees, all of which were available for anyone to view on the Ancestry websites.

[Here I must interject a plea for all who go to the trouble of creating a family tree on Ancestry or similar sites not to hide it from public view. It is only by letting others see what we have discovered that we can further our own research. Family history is a mutual help pastime. The interchange of names, sources and background data enables everyone's tree to flourish and expand. It also helps correct the many errors that inevitably result from copying without checking or confirming sources. To hide one's tree while freely gathering information from those who provide public access is to act no better than the robber barons of our past].

It was these emails that eventually led to major personal lifestyle disruptions. Late in a life of many changes and upheavals, I became seduced by still more changes that awaited, with fresh paths to travel. And even now, several years on, there remain some that I have not yet fully accepted nor adjusted to.

One of these life-changing emails, as mentioned in an earlier chapter, revealed the hitherto unknown existence of the woman called Lynne, who boldly claimed us to be cousins, a fact since supported by various DNA tests. Her probing into the past had taken her back to Wales in the 1840s where she found one of her line had hitched up with one of my line. Three generations later, wrote Lynne, we were entwined as cousins. Thus began a journey that both of us had only vaguely considered and which, until she pressed the Send button, we had been destined to travel alone.

Vying with Lynne's emails for my newly-aroused interest in my family's history were those that began arriving from Heather in Bournemouth. She, too, greeted me as 'cousin' and provided a wealth of documentation to show all the links to this relationship.

Our continuing communication has been less frequent but every bit as detailed. It also has that same element of friendliness and humour that makes such contacts so enjoyable. Despite its rather spasmodic nature, it has endured through numerous long silences mostly caused by other preoccupations and the demands of daily life. We are friends, we are family and, although it took more than a decade before we met, we have attained that level of closeness that raises family history way above the mere gathering of names and dates.

The information received from Heather indicated meticulous research and a sense of order for which I continually strive but have yet to attain. Over the years, this has proved a continual blessing. She kindly points to my errors and offers corrections, always supported by her reasoning and her sources. Reliability is in the detail.

It was Heather who first drew my attention to lighthouseman Charles Edwin Nicholas, the son of my great-grand-aunt, Agness Berry of Milford Haven, and merchant seaman Thomas Nicholas.

It was she who brought to light the details mentioned earlier: that not only had Charles served as a keeper at the Wolf Rock light, set on a sea-battered outcrop between Land's End and the Scilly Isles but, while stationed at this isolated guardian of the shipping lanes, had somehow found time and opportunity to court and marry a Cornish girl with the wonderful name, among others, of Sidonia, and had subsequently served at the famed Lizard Light on Britain's southernmost tip.

Thanks to Heather, Charles emerged from obscurity as a mere name among many to become that figure referred to in crime dramas as, 'a person of interest.' And provided my unexpected ancestral link to the Celtic nations of Wales (Cymru) and Cornwall (Kernow).

However, the result of further probing had left me with an unsatisfactory conclusion. I strongly suspected it painted Charles in a far poorer light than he deserved but could not prove otherwise. The timeline contained an enormously large gap and it was too easy to draw conclusions that were way off the mark from the information then uncovered.

Was he really such an uncaring and absentee husband and father as this data could imply? Somehow, I doubted it and certainly did not wish it to be so.

I needed to know more…

A COLONIAL CAREER

BACK ON THE RESEARCH trail, I found that 22 April 1892 not only marked the death of Charles and Sidonia's son, Charles Claude, but was also the day the 2280-tonne *Diomed* sailed out of Liverpool for Hong Kong.

Primarily a cargo ship ploughing along at a mere ten knots between the UK and the Far East, the *Diomed* was carrying only five passengers, one of whom was a Mr C Nicholas listed as 'single'. The others on board were a Mr and Mrs J Mitchell and a Mr and Mrs F Coleman. Trinity House records reveal that lighthouse keepers named Joseph Mitchell and Francis A Coleman had served with Charles at his various postings. Like him, they had also resigned in April 1892 to join the Hong Kong Lighthouse Service.

It therefore seemed safe to assume that passenger Mr C Nicholas was 'my' Charles. But it was also galling and depressing to have to accept that he had left his Cornish wife and family living with her parents in Landewednack.

Everything suggested they had split up – she a true Cornish home-body and he a young man with career ambitions and a chance to see the world. Also, by being described as 'single' on the *Diomed*'s passenger list, he seemed to be denying his married status, although this now seems to have been a shipping company clerk's indication that he was travelling alone or was allotted a single cabin.

The overriding impression gained from the records then available was that he was running away from a depressing home life of sickness and infant deaths in the hope of success and fortune. The Hong Kong Light-house Service was in its infancy, building new lights and offering exciting opportunities for experienced keepers from Britain.

For Charles, such prospects would be a sharp contrast to the demands of a familiar routine and a domestic situation that saw three of his six children die in infancy. Any career advancement within Trinity House would inevitably mean moving from the Lizard, so one remote location within England or Wales would have seemed to Sidonia as unappealing as any other.

With Charles now far away, death certificates for sons Charles Wesley (1891) and Charles Claude (1892) state it was grandfather Frances Jose who had the unpleasant task of being 'present at the death' of the two infants. Cousin Charles could thus so easily be painted as a ne'er do well shirking family responsibilities. After all, jumping to conclusions is a prime activity of many who indulge in tracing their ancestors.

In Charles' case, it was difficult not to imagine a husband who perhaps felt let down by a wife who refused to accompany him on his Hong Kong venture (unlike the wives of his colleagues) and who preferred the comfort and care of her family and the close-knit community on the windswept Lizard headland.

On reflection, however, Charles could equally well be a man willing to sacrifice a home life in his determination to get on in the world and ensure a steady income and a comfortable retirement for himself and his wife.

From the time Charles sailed off to Hong Kong, it was his in-laws, Francis and Jane Champion Jose (nee Gilbert), who provided a home for Sidonia. In the 1901 census she was recorded as living at the parental home, Green Cottage, with daughter Elaine Sidonia (born in 1897) and one of their twin boys, Francis Norman. The other twin, Percival Thomas, was boarding at a private school run by Irish couple William and Elizabeth Wagner at 3 Station Villas, Phillack.

Although small, the school had among its scholars two brothers from Canterbury and two from France. This presented another conundrum: were the fees paid by Francis Jose to compensate his daughter for deciding to remain in Cornwall, or was the distant Charles now earning and saving at a much improved level and remitting money from Hong

> **Hayle Grammar School.**
>
> HEAD MASTER : —
> MR. W. WAGNER, LONDON UNIVERSITY.
> RESIDENT ASSISTANT :—MR. J. H. C. DUNN.
> *Shorthand Teacher :—*
> MR. G. T. COCK (Honorsman,) F.N.P.S
> DRILL INSTRUCTOR : — SERGEANT KENT.
> SUCCESSES gained at London, Dublin, the Royal, and Aberdeen Universities, Oxford Senior and Junior, Cambridge Junior, College of Preceptors, Preliminary Pharmaceutical and Law, Engineer Students' Open Competition (17th, 19th and 31st positions,) and Open Scholarship at Newton College.
> BOARDERS RECEIVED.
> 23 Successes (13 in Shorthand) recently obtained. Next Term commenced January 15th.

Percival's school advertises in The Cornishman, 25 January 1894

Kong, thus indicating another reason for his move to the distant colony?

By the time of the 1911 census, only Elaine was still living with her mother in Landewednack and Percival had emigrated to Canada. There he found work as a carpenter and married a single mother from North Dakota. He served in World War I as a bandsman with the Canadian Expeditionary Force and later moved to Minnesota. There he progressed into becoming a house builder and contractor, eventually fathering at least seven children, one of whom bore the name Sidonia. (But more of Percy and his eventually troubled and troublesome life later).

Francis was by then boarding in Woolwich, London, while working as an instrument maker. He married Hannah Broad Newman on the outbreak of war in 1914 and they later settled in Nuneaton, Warwickshire, where he died in the local hospital in 1952.

Lighthouse-keeper and husband Charles appears on neither census. This suggested a lengthy, even permanent, sojourn in Hong Kong and the need for more research in the former Crown colony and at Trinity House. It was still difficult to accept that this ostensibly hard-working and decent man, who had put time and effort into courting the woman upon who he lavished expensive gifts, could be such a callous charlatan as to desert her and their brood without worthy cause.

One glimmer of light in my negative findings was that he apparently showed enough concern for his wife and children as to endure at least a couple of long and tedious voyages from and to Hong Kong to visit his family in Cornwall.

Although his name is absent from any incoming passenger records, a Mr C E Nicholas was listed as sailing out of London for Hong Kong on the *Sunda* (or *Lunda*) on 21 October 1896 and on the *Marmora* on 17 February 1904.

Both dates are significant. It was six months after the first of these 'visits' that Elaine Agnes Sidonia Nicholas was born at the Landewednack home with Charles registered as the father. And it was in October 1903, a few months before the second departure, that the couple's last child, Bertram Charles, was born only to die on 22 December as the result of a premature birth but, most significantly, with 'Charles Nicholas, father, present at the death'.

Apart from that confirmation on Bertram's death certificate of his presence in Cornwall and his spasmodic appearance on passenger lists, Charles left not a trace of UK residency after leaving Dungeness lighthouse and Trinity House employ in 1892 until he suddenly re-emerges in the early 1930s living in retirement in Hertfordshire.

For a long while, and through many hours of searching, the lives of Sidonia and Charles remained a mystery around which could be woven all manner of domestic situations; she continuing to live in the home of her parents on the edge of the desolate village green in Landewednack and him steaming back and forth between Hong Kong and the UK – a long and tedious journey far from the easy commute it has become in the era of the jumbo jet.

But, as ever in the world of the family historian, persistence pays …

If researchers are to enliven a bland list of dates and names and inject some life and interest into their forebears' existence they need to adopt the attitude of a Jack Russell. They must chew on the 'bones' of the past until they are sucked dry – and, even then, keep on gnawing away. A Jack Russell is not content with a tennis ball but must rip it into innumerable pieces and discover what lies within.

Thus it was with Charles and Sidonia Nicholas. When I set their file aside for a year or more I knew only part of their story had been unravelled. Everything gathered so far indicated there was still much more to discover.

When I eventually returned to their tree I also turned to Google, an indispensable and ever-expanding resource for every researcher, and focused on Hong Kong and its lighthouses. The trail led me to the Royal Asiatic Society and a paper presented to one of the society's regular lectures titled *Hong Kong's Lighthouses and the Men Who Manned Them*. It was one of those Eureka moments beloved of family historians.

The paper revealed Hong Kong had begun setting up a modern lighthouse service only as recently as the late nineteenth century, the very time when Charles had handed in his resignation to Trinity House.

In 1867, Commander Reed, a naval surveyor, had proposed the small islands of Waglan and Gap Rock, to the south of Hong Kong Island, as suitable locations for lighthouses to cover the port approaches. However, as neither was within Hong Kong waters, it was not until 1892 and 1893, after much intense negotiation between Hong Kong and China, that the proposed lighthouses were built.

The two governments agreed Gap Rock lighthouse would be built by the British and maintained by them, but the island would remain Chinese territory not to be used for any other purpose. The light first beamed forth in April 1892 using equipment built in Sweden.

When, three years later the lantern was smashed by a severe typhoon, experts said the lighthouse should have been built on the northern part of the rock instead of the southern part. But because of the cost to rebuild it, the original light continued to function through forty years of typhoons until the Japanese invasion in 1941.

From this initial discovery I was taken on a merry-go-round of Hong Kong Government departments that eventually provided a link to *HK Government Reports Online – Civil Establishment of Hong Kong Year by Year*, an archive listing in great detail everybody who worked for the colony's government. And there among the hundreds of names was the elusive Charles Nicholas, one of the first to apply and be appointed to the new lighthouse service.

His initial posting was from 25 April 1892 as keeper at the Gap Rock lighthouse under the control of the Hong Kong Harbourmaster's office. He was paid an annual salary of $HK1020 and had two British assistants and three local Chinese assistants.

Gap Rock is a barren dot in the ocean. It consists of two hillocks, about 80 to 100 feet high. The lighthouse rose nearly 50 feet, setting the light about 142 feet above mean sea level. Nonetheless, in heavy storms seas broke right over the lighthouse with Charles and his companions huddled inside.

These records show every pay rise (and deduction) and all leave taken throughout Charles' employment. Entries such as the one stating that from 1 March to 31 December 1903 *'Mr C E Nicholas drew half salary while on leave and the remainder of his salary was drawn by Mr Peter Jackson, temporary lightkeeper'.* On his return, his salary was increased to $HK1800 a year.

It was a life of rugged, almost primitive living conditions and long hours interspersed with lengthy periods of home leave with pay cut by half. Here at last was an indication of how Charles and Sidonia sustained their relationship, with Charles remaining in Hong Kong, now as principal keeper at the Waglan Island light, through most of World War I.

He was recorded as 'absent from Colony' for two months during 1916 and 'retired on pension' on 21 June 1917 at the age of 55, when he presumably returned to the UK and, for some reason then still to be discovered, not to Cornwall but to St Albans in Hertfordshire, which is about as far as he could get from the wild shores on which he had spent so much of his life.

Living there with him was the ever-faithful Mary Ann Sidonia. Some-how, despite the infant deaths, break-ups and long absences, they had come full circle and were back together thirty years on from those troubled times on the Lizard.

The Gap Rock light in 1893

Sidonia shared Charles' retirement until his death from 'heart failure, myocardial degeneration and herniplegia' on 8 April 1930. She lived on until 24 September 1938, bequeathing her effects valued at £571 4s 4d to their daughter, and my second cousin, Elaine Agnes Sidonia Nicholas, who married Ernest Ranner in Helston in 1919, thus providing yet more threads to be woven into my Cornish ancestry.

Of the couple's two other children to survive beyond a few months, first-born Francis Norman moved to Woolwich in London as an appren-tice instrument maker, married the girl next door and died in hospital in Nuneaton, Warwickshire on 4 July 1952 age 66, and Percival Thomas (of whom more later) set sail for America as a teenager and eventually settled as a carpenter in Minnesota, where he died on 8 July 1944 age 58.

And that was that, or so I thought.

Surprisingly, however, more information suddenly arrived that led to a fresh trail of enquiry which, thanks to input from recently discovered cousin Heather, finally tied up all the loose ends and provided the con-cluding chapter to this story of a Cornish maid's enduring love.

But first, an explanatory interlude.

MY MAN IN HONG KONG

IT WAS ANOTHER OF those 'out of the blue' moments that help make family history such a delight and a source of continual surprises. An email arrived with the salutation 'Dear Mr Bee', which alone was enough to attract my attention ahead of all the dross that daily clutters the inbox.

Even more intriguing, its sender signed off as S W Poon, adjunct professor in the University of Hong Kong's department of real estate and construction – not my usual field of interest by any means.

Professor Poon, or SW as he soon became known, had spent three years leading research into Hong Kong's heritage lighthouses. This included trying to track down the keepers of the lights and their stories. The local branch of the Royal Asiatic Society had informed him of my interest in Charles Nicholas.

As part of his research, SW had discovered that a diary written by Charles detailing life and conditions throughout his years in Hong Kong was now in the possession of his great-granddaughter, Sylvia.

SW had tried to contact her to seek access to the diary but had received no reply. He hoped I could help as *'the diary must have included lot of invaluable information such as the start of the Gap Rock lighthouse, including the damage due to severe storms after the light was lit.'*

This was the first I had heard about the diary, which could well unravel much of the mystery surrounding Charles' decision to move to Hong Kong. It was also likely to provide much more detail about his trips back home to Cornwall.

Thus began a fresh round of detective work, which saw the addition of several more names to my family tree, eventually coming right up to the present by locating Charles Nicholas's great-great-grandson, a business analyst running his own company in London. All this I passed on to SW.

Meanwhile, all this activity had, to use an Australian expression, stirred the possum with the result that cousin Heather had taken a fresh look at her own research. Her focus was now on our other shared link – Charles' wife Sidonia and all the other Joses gathered around the Lizard.

Sidonia, one of the rarest of female names, is one that has been attached to Heather's grandmother, mother, sister and a cousin in the US. Family lore says it comes from Medina Sidonia, leader of the Spanish Armada. But its roots lie many centuries further back in the ancient Mediterranean port of Sidon, where a local woman would have been known as a Sidonia. Phœnicians from Sidon probably founded the Andalusian city of Medina-Sidonia in southern Spain. The medieval dukedom of Medina-Sidonia still exists with the title held by the controversial aristocrat Luisa Isabel Álvarez de Toledo until her death in 2008.

As Heather and I have discovered, researching the Jose lines is fraught with almost as many confusions, uncertainties and duplications as confront someone delving into a Smith, Jones or Brown tree.

The Joses are prolific. Their trails led us down as many burrows as riddled by rabbits on the headlands of the Lizard peninsular. Simply trying to sort one John Jose from another is a jigsaw which nearly always seems to have at least one piece missing.

It does not help that while some, such as Sidonia's family, appeared to be highly respected and respectable members of the community, others clearly tended to be less so. Fights, thefts, adultery, bastardy, family disputes and general lawlessness are constant and frequent features of their record.

While most remained firmly rooted in a corner of Cornwall that must have been a truly wild west throughout most of the nineteenth century, others flitted around the globe, some at their own whim and others dispatched by the courts.

What they and their histories provide is a hugely varied and colourful tapestry. To visit the Lizard, and the wilder the weather the better, is to be caught up in a swirl of emotions. The spirits of this often turbulent clan are never far away. The headlands, cliffs, coves, churchyards, memorials and moors seem little touched by the twenty-first century, providing an unchanged and unchanging backdrop to the shades of my kinfolk eddying around me.

The Celtic lure, here as in Wales, is a powerful and mysterious force. And now it is time to meet some of the 'family'…

SHEEP-STEALERS, THIEVES AND KILLERS

ONLY WHEN I TOOK a closer look at what I had hitherto considered to be merely vague connections to Cornwall did the darker side of my Lizard Peninsula ancestors begin to unfold.

The marriage of my Welsh ancestor Charles Nicholas to Lizard resident Mary Ann Sidonia Jose had already led my research to embrace Sidonia's wider Jose family. It was thus that the focus fell on two ne'er-do-wells, Stephen Jose (born in Mullion on 23 October 1808) and his elder brother James Jose (born in Breage about 1801).

It was soon obvious that James was far from being a good role model for his younger brothers. His criminal record began early. In 1818, at the age of 17, he was sentenced to six months' imprisonment for larceny - and he never improved, although in January 1828 he did gain acquittal on another larceny charge.

It was in early 1829 when things went seriously wrong for these two Jose men and, reading between the lines of various newspaper reports, what happened on the night of Wednesday 18 February was merely one more incident in a string of criminal acts.

As the *Royal Cornwall Guardian* put it, the windswept moorlands around Helston and Meneage had for several years been infested by a gang of thieves '*who have carried out their system of plunder to an extent which has been seldom if ever equalled*'.

The newspaper claimed hardly a farmer in the area had escaped being robbed. But there was violence, too, for '*such has been the terror in which they have been held that they chose rather to submit to be robbed with impunity than run the risk of an unsuccessful search, which would have brought upon them the vengeance of these miscreants*'.

Among these 'miscreants' (surely a rather too gentle term for scaring the living daylights out of the local community) were two of my relatives, the Jose brothers.

When a farmer by the name of Silvester, living half a mile from Helston, had four high-bred rams stolen (one of them a Kerrier Show prize-winner) he procured warrants for searches of the Landewednack . premises of James Jose along with those of Henry Harris and Alexander Hocking at Grade. The newspaper reported that nothing was found at the latter two places apart from two legs and some skins at the premises occupied by Hocking, a butcher.

At James Jose's place the search revealed eighty-two pounds of mutton cut up into small chunks and salted. This had been concealed in a bed-tye *which from size and description left but little doubt of being part of the largest sheep*.

James Jose and Alexander Hocking were arrested and sent to Helston where Hocking immediately set about proving there's no honour among thieves by providing sufficient information to justify a search party setting out to arrest James's brother. Stephen, along with William Harris and several other suspects.

Eventually there were forty or more people clambering over the cliffs and searching the coast's many caves. This is challenging and forbidding terrain even in the best of weather but in early February it would have been extremely inhospitable to pursuers and pursued alike, with Constable Andrew from Helston reportedly ensuring all possible escape routes were covered.

Jose and Hocking were eventually seen crossing the open land above Kynance Cove where they were headed off by local farmers Hendy and (another) Hocking. They fled back towards the cove and, in a move that smacks of reckless and unthinking desperation, plunged into the sea - this at night in the middle of winter.

Farmer Hocking shouted and pleaded with the men to turn back but *after swimming about twenty minutes they were seen to sink to rise no more*.

Constable Andrew ran two miles to the nearest cove – an admirable feat of fitness and endurance, as anyone familiar with that landscape will attest - to procure a boat, but by the time he returned to Kynance the escapees had disappeared *and nothing but their hats were picked up*.

The search party found the skin of Mr Silvester's largest ram in one of the caves. It had been cut into several pieces. Three other men were later tracked down and taken into custody in Helston. After being brought before local justice John Borlase, with Hocking turning up as witness for the prosecution, they were dismissed with 'an admonition', an astonishingly lenient verdict in an era renowned for harsh justice and severe sentencing.

James Jose, however, did not enjoy such leniency and was committed for trial, again with Hocking called to appear against him. A further sentencing surprise ensued when a plea of not guilty was accepted and Jose was acquitted. Perhaps the loss of his brother was considered sufficient penalty.

However, the acquittal failed to act as a deterrent. Within three years James was back in court, this time at the Cornwall Quarter Sessions in Bodmin after being sent for trial by Justice Borlase.

He was charged with entering the barn of Landewednack farmer Samuel Chittock and stealing a quantity of barley. This time there was no acquittal, no reprieve or admonishment. He was found guilty and sentenced to transportation to New South Wales for fourteen years.

That could well have been the making of him. When he arrived in Sydney on the *Isabella* on 13 February 1832 the notes against his name stated, '*No pardon, no ticket of leave, no certificate of freedom*'. This document, and several others, also stated his sentence to be 'life' rather than fourteen years.

With him on the voyage were seven others who had been convicted at either the assizes or the quarter sessions in Cornwall: William Downing (sentenced to seven years), Nicholas Wallis (fourteen years), Francis Dorrington and Joseph Smith (seven), William Plomer (seven), John William Bloxham (seven) and Thomas Grady (life).

He served his time – periods of it in North Parramatta Gaol for reasons so far undiscovered - and received several tickets of leave.

Eventually a Convict Application to Marry was submitted and granted to allow him to wed Jane Curtis (or Carr) on 27 January 1843 at the prestigious Scots Church in Sydney. His bride, a forty-five-year-old widow, was a free emigrant.

On 20 February 1948 James was granted a conditional pardon. He and Jane continued to live in Parramatta until his death in 1875, probably eventually enjoying a better, and less lawless, life than if he had remained on the Lizard.

Back home, other members of the Jose families continued their often-troubled ways.

The worst incident involved Jeremiah Jose who lived at Gunwalloe and various places in the Mullion area, including the family farm at Trenance Vean.

He appeared at Cornwall Assizes in 1827 on a charge of having killed his nephew, Francis Jose '*in a fit of rage*'. Or, as the headstone over Francis's grave in Mullion churchyard puts it rather more poetically:

> *His life was taken from the earth*
> *Not by burning fever nor pining sickness.*
> *A hand which should have fostered did the fatal deed,*
> *And by a nail transfixed he staggered, fell and died.*

An even more graphic version of events was given in court where it was explained the fatal act occurred during '*a period of great excitement, caused by a quarrel*' that led to Francis calling his uncle 'an old rogue'.

Jeremiah inexplicably took a nail from his pocket and plunged it into the young man's temple. When told he had killed his nephew he was claimed to have said, '*If I have done it, I'd give a room full of gold to restore him again*'.

The jury remained unmoved by his contrition and found him guilty of manslaughter. He was sentenced to be transported for life but a mitigation plea resulted in this being commuted to a mere two years' imprisonment.

He later returned to Trenance Vean, where he died on 2 January 1845. His wife Mary (nee Oates), who he married on 27 July 1794, died two years later on 29 September 1847.

The name Jeremiah Jose lived on, passing down through at least two more generations with respectability eventually being restored to the family when the next Jeremiah - who farmed ninety acres, employed three men and two boys and had a household servant and child's maid - not only served on the local council but also as a juryman in the same assize court that had once handed his father a life sentence in Australia.

Although the numerous Joses living on the Lizard peninsular are off-shoots from the main branches of my tree, we are nonetheless linked and, like other relatives I have discovered, they help confirm the sense of Cornishness that has always lurked in the background.

When research such as written about here goes beyond the basic listing of names and dates, our ancestors become people rather than statistics. By delving deeper into the many resources now available we open a window into lives that were so often harder and harsher than anything we face today.

Yet they survived, often being accepted back into the community against which they had transgressed and even sinned …

FRANCIS THE FORNICATOR

ON THE LAST SUNDAY of August 1774, Gunwalloe resident Francis Jose stood outside Mullion Church, a chastened and humbled man. It was a dreary and dull day with tornados and floods reported further up country after an earlier period of extreme heat - a bit like the recent times and suggesting climate change is far from a new phenomenon. What happened next can only be imagined, based on creased and yellowing documents seen at the Cornwall Record Office.

Francis took off his hat and placed it on the bench inside the church porch. Slowly he removed his shoes and hose and placed them alongside his shoes. He rolled up his trousers to bare his legs. Finally, he unrolled a long swathe of white cloth and draped it carefully over one shoulder, ensuring its folds fell almost to the ground.

Churchwardens Thomas Shepherd and William Hendy stood impassively alongside, noting and checking each move. No smiles or familiar greetings were exchanged.

Mr Shepherd gave Francis a white rod to hold in his right hand. Satisfied all was as it should be, Mr Hendy slowly opened the door, anxious not to make a noise to disturb the congregation within.

As the minister, John Passmore, came to the end of the reading of the second lesson the churchwardens signalled Francis to move forward down the aisle. They fell into step behind him. Slowly he shuffled towards the minister's desk, the floor's polished flagstones cold to his feet, eyes turning to watch his progress.

The reading of the Nicene Creed was about to begin but not until Francis had stopped in front of the minister, a churchwarden at either shoulder. Everyone stood with heads bowed until the prayer's end and the congregation had echoed the minister's 'Amen'.

There was a numbing and expectant silence. The minister nodded at Francis - a cue for him to begin what he had been instructed to do 'in an audible voice'. The words he spoke had been ordered by a sitting of the Archdeaconry Court of Cornwall:

> '*I Francis Jose do humbly confess and acknowledge that I have highly offended Almighty God by committing the foul sin of adultery and being thereby so great a scandal to the church of Christian religion for which I do declare my hearty sorrow and penitence and here in the presence of Almighty God and before this congregation promise by God's assistance amendment of self for the future beseeching God to pardon me and desiring you to pray for me.*'

At the end, Francis sank to his knees and repeated the Lord's Prayer, again 'in an audible voice'. His duty was done, his penitence complete, and he was escorted back down the aisle by the churchwardens and two local residents, William Freeman and Charles Dales, aware of all his neighbours' eyes upon him. It would have been a shaming and humbling experience.

All that remained was for the minister, the churchwardens and the two residents to sign a certificate attesting that penance had been performed and which Frances was to present to the archdeaconry court 'on or before the ninth day of September next ensuing'.

Francis, a distant relative born in Wendron on 28 December 1735 and found clinging to the outer branches of my family tree, was married to Jane Morrish (or Morice) when he committed 'the foul sin of adultery'. In the formal words of the court, he had confessed to '*being the sworn father of a base child by one Elizabeth Wedlock late of the same parish spinster.*'

His paramour, aged twenty-four at the time of their fornication, was born in Wendron on New Year's Day 1751 to

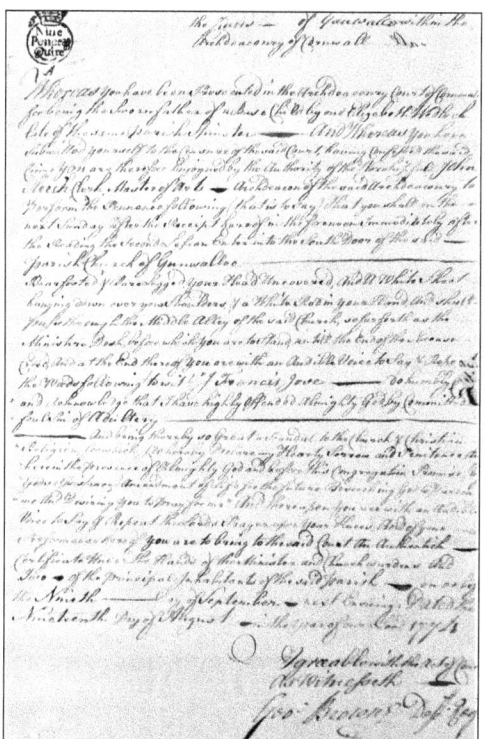

The archdeacon's penance order on Francis Jose

James and Blanch Wedlock but no reliable records have so far been found of the child of this sinful liaison. Information sourced from the Cornwall Online Parish Clerks' database does however show that an Elizabeth Wedlock married blacksmith Joseph Roberts in Gulval on 11 February 1797.

What appears to be this same couple registered the birth of daughter Elizabeth *Wedlock* Roberts (the clue's in the name!) in Gulval on 27 July 1800. Unfortunately, any joy Elizabeth might have garnered from her late-life respectability was short-lived as she died in Gulval on 7 December 1801 at the age of 51.

Meanwhile, Francis seemingly became reconciled with wife Jane and went on to father more children by her and to share with her a grave that remains in the grounds surrounding the church where he took his walk of shame.

Jane was the first to die, buried on 1 May 1805. Francis Joseph followed four years later on 13 January 1809. Perhaps he was the one who decided on the inscription written on their tombstone; certainly, it takes on pertinent and fresh meaning when the story of Francis's indiscretion is known:

Headstone over the grave in Mullion churchyard of Jane and Francis Jose

> *Within this place our bodies mouldering lie*
> *Reader consider that thou too shall die.*
> *Be wise in time, repent and pardon crave*
> *For there is no repentance in the grave.*
> *Then you like us is redeemed to Heaven fly*
> *And at life's exit shout the victory.*

OTHER COUSIN JACKS

Soon after I began delving into the Cornish connections created by the marriage of Welsh cousin Charles Edwin Nicholas to Landewednack lass Sidonia Jose - I realised I had entered a genealogical maze.

That cliched phrase 'a tight-knit community' hardly did it justice. This was so tight-knit, and the Jose name so prolific, as to be akin to a skein of wool attacked by a basket of playful kittens. Unravelling it with any certainty would be a challenge like that faced by anyone researching the surnames Smith, Brown or Jones. Ahead lay a path strewn with doubts and uncertainties where obtaining conclusive proof the correct ancestor had been found would be almost impossible for many of them.

Like others of earlier times, the Joses bred large families and stayed close to home. Most of them stayed deeply entrenched within the sea-washed confines of the Lizard Peninsula which, even today, presents as a singular attachment to the rest of Cornwall; remote, cloistered and self-contained.

Among the many stay-at homes there were, however, a few who broke loose and ventured far afield. Most went of their own accord but one or two, already mentioned, were dispatched at the order of the courts. The majority remained in their new homelands and founded Jose dynasties, although a couple did make it back to English shores.

One of the youngest to quit the Lizard was cousin John Jose, determined to start a new life after some turbulent years at home. His father had died when John was only four-years-old and his sister, Elizabeth, had followed their father six months later after living only three months. John's mother, Elizabeth (nee Harry) had since formed a liaison with a Mr Secombe (or Seccombe, the most likely candidate being Thomas Seccombe, a married cordwainer from nearby Mawgan-in-Meneage) and given birth to an illegitimate daughter, Isabella, who lived for a mere six months.

But the biggest setback came in 1838 when his older brother, Richard, died at sea while aboard the Royal Navy brigantine *Skylark*. The ship, built in Pembroke (another Cornwall-Wales link) and commissioned in 1831, was stationed at Falmouth.

Little wonder, therefore, that migration held great appeal for the unfortunate John. When he arrived in Quebec, Canada, at the end of the 1830s, he was barely out of his teens. At some stage of his journey (was this a shipboard romance?) he met Scottish lass Jane Vance, from Glen Luche, a place so far not found on any map but reliably mentioned in the family's records and folklore. On 7 May 1840, when Jane was still only sixteen years old, they were married at St John's Presbyterian Church in Quebec City.

The newlyweds soon moved to Toronto where they lived to the end of their days with Jane's death, at the age of ninety-two in July 1915, being reported in the local newspapers as that of 'one of Toronto's oldest residents who had settled in the city before the coming of the railroads'.

In memory of John's brother they named their first son Richard who fittingly was a lone survivor among the couple's early days of parenting. Their first-born, Elizabeth in 1844, had lived less than three months but was remembered first in another Elizabeth, who lived barely two years from 1853 to 1855, and yet again on 25 August 1856 with Elizabeth Jane, who bucked the trend and lived to the age of eighty-seven.

Another early death was that of John, who survived for only six weeks from birth in January 1849 and was remembered a year later when another boy was born and given the name of John.

The family's fortunes vastly improved from the birth of the third Elizabeth with most of the surviving seven children, marrying, having children and living to a ripe old age. The one setback was Sarah, born in 1866 and who married late at the age of thirty-nine but lived for only another four years.

And so, to the best of my knowledge, at least one twiglet on the Jose family tree has put down deep roots and continues to grow and thrive in Canada.

Some sixty or so years after John Jose set out from his home on the Lizard to try his luck on the other side of the Atlantic, another teenager from the Jose clan was planning to follow in his footsteps. And for much the same reason, as he tried to explain to his hapless mother.

'But Ma, life here is so depressing,' whinged young Percy Nicholas as he helped his mother in the kitchen of the solid grey-washed four-square Green Cottage facing the windswept village green at Landewednack. 'It's all death and gloom.'

'Learn your books and get a trade,' she chided him. 'You're young, things will get better.'

'How can you of all people say that?'

His mother didn't need to ask what he meant. The memories were always well to the fore.

Sidonia Jose, as she was before marrying lighthouse-keeper Charles Nicholas, had found life a tough struggle since the heady, happy days of courtship and the grand wedding. She needed little reminding of the three births, two boys and a girl, in three years with the daughter dying after only nine months. Two more sons died within months before she at last gave birth to a healthy daughter. And for much of this time hus-band Charles had been absent on distant postings, usually when he was most needed.

She recalled the time she tried accompanying him on one of his postings – to the lighthouse on the shingled English Channel shore of the windswept Romney Marshes at Dungeness but had soon scut-tled back home, depressed by the bleak and remote location known by many as Britain's only desert, such is its barren and sandy con-stitution. Even today, despite all the inroads made upon other wil-derness areas, it remains as desolate and exposed to the elements as it would have been during Charles' posting there. It is a place of

Dungeness Lighthouse looms over the round house that was home to the light's keepers, Charles Edwin Nicholas and family included.

scattered shacks, abandoned fishing boats, flotsam and driftwood, all incessantly battered by Channel gales and overlooked by the ominous looming presence of the huge Dungeness B nuclear plant.

The huddle of solid stone cottages clustered at the foot of the phallic form of the Dungeness Light, miles from any other habitation or convenience, was where the pregnant Sidonia had to make a home for herself, Charles and their two young sons, Percy and Francis. Her only companion and solace had been Charles's sister, Ada, filling the role of governess. At least back on the Lizard she and her family were part of a strong community, no matter how isolated it might be from the rest of Cornwall.

It had been after Charles completed his tour of duty at Dungeness that he informed Sidonia he had decided to seize the opportunity to join the newly formed lighthouse service in faraway Hong Kong.

'It's for the better,' he tried to convince her. 'Better money and I'll get long leave breaks, so it won't be much different from if I was being posted to lights around England.'

Sidonia had reluctantly agreed and now had to face up to having son Percy move far away across the sea.

With husband Charles in distant Hong Kong, Sidonia now lived in her parents' home with her children, Francis, Percy and Elaine, and was recovering from yet another infant death, her fifth son. In such circumstances she could well understand what young Percy meant when he announced he, too, was going to chase opportunities far from the Lizard.

'I've got to get away, there's nothing here for me,' Percy insisted. 'It's cutting and polishing the stone, or fishing or farming.'

Sidonia sighed. Her family were all stone-cutters, spending hours at the wheel to shape and polish the unique local blue-grey serpentine rock. It was all they ever knew apart from hard graft as agricultural labourers. Her eldest son, Francis, had already rejected such a future and decided he would be better off elsewhere. He had made his way to London and settled into regular employment as an instrument maker. Now it was happening all over again.

She knew there was little she could say to persuade Percy to stay. She could understand his unhappiness, some of which stemmed from having been a reluctant boarder at the nascent Hayle Grammar School, several miles away on the north Cornwall coast at Phillack.

There Percy lived in the home of an Irish couple, the school's headmaster William Wagner and his wife Elizabeth. Living under the same roof were the Wagners' three teenage children, assistant teacher William James Griff and three fellow 'scholars' who came from Ireland, Yorkshire and Wales. It was situation of 'them and us', with the four students very much on the downside of a rigorous routine and harsh living conditions.

'Why so far? Why America?' pleaded Sidonia. It was the playing of a last desperate card. If he had to go, perhaps he could at least remain in England like Francis had done.

But he was not to be dissuaded. Eventually, Sidonia faced the inevitable and, in 1906, at the age of 19, my cousin Percy boarded the SS *Baltic* in Liverpool and joined hundreds of other hopefuls making the transatlantic crossing to the USA.

Thus was grafted another branch on to my family tree.

Percy did not hang about. Within a few years he had taken on the role of father to Victor Wilbur Runyon, born on 14 January 1909 to unmarried Dorothy (or Dolly, as she became known) Gladys Runyon who was working as a servant in the household of a widowed farmer deep in Amish country in the farming community of West Union, Minnesota.

In the 1910 US Census, Victor Walter is recorded as 'son of Miss Dolly [sic] Runyon' and that his unnamed father's home state was North Dakota. Although Dolly was born in North Dakota, her parents were from Minnesota and the family had returned there some time before the birth of Victor Wilbur.

How and where she and Percy met remains a mystery as that same US census makes no mention of Percy. He was then in Canada, working sixty hours a week as a carpenter while living in a boarding house in Strathcona, Alberta, run by Fred and Elizabeth Archer and crammed with migrant workers.

But at some stage love eventually triumphed and Dolly and Victor Wilbur travelled from Minnesota – the verdant border state of 10,000 lakes - to share Percy's rugged lifestyle on Canada's frontier land.

Strathcona was a rough and newly-settled town. It had grown rapidly thanks to a sudden influx of land speculators, fur traders, pioneer farmers, hunters, general hangers-on and hopeful sub-contractors such as Percy. Its polyglot community consisted mainly of immigrants from Britain (especially the Orkney Isles), almost every European country, the USA and other parts of Canada.

Strathcona's main street c. 1909
[Creative Commons licence, University of Alberta digitalisation project]

Residents lived in hastily-built primitive shacks and log cabins which were gradually replaced by more substantial two-storey wood or even brick buildings, many of which exist today.

Conditions were much the same in the many other communities growing up throughout this pioneering region, with the building of railways rapidly providing opportunities for trade and exploration.

Ever in pursuit of work, Percy soon moved a few miles south to Wetaskiwin, named after a Cree word meaning 'the hills where peace was made' – where the warring Blackfoot and Cree tribes resolved to end their fighting.

Set at 2490 ft amid lakes and sandy hills on what was once the coast of the large sea that covered much of Alberta millions of years ago Wetaskiwin is one of Alberta's oldest cities, founded in 1892. The temperature can drop to -18C in winter and averages only in the mid-20s in summer.

It was here, on 1 April 1912, that Percy married Dolly and took on the responsibility of being a father to the illegitimate Victor. He was now the breadwinner and the need for work took them to lakeside Le Duc, a similar but even younger township, which saw its first settlers in the 1890s.

Here, in November 1913, Dolly gave birth to their first daughter, who they significantly named Sidonia. It was here, too, that they were for the first time recorded as a family unit, all bearing the surname of Nicholas and with Percy and Dolly listed as 'married'.

All are also stated to be of Canadian nationality and of English birth. These details, listed in a record of a US border crossing in November 1913 - have all the signs of being hastily completed by a less than scrupulous official; a far cry from today's rigorous procedures.

Conditions in Canada's pioneering backwoods had become all too much for Dolly. Too parched and dry in summer, too cold and windswept in winter, more brown than green despite the forests edging the wide plains. And she was homesick.

'Can we go back home?' pleaded Dolly. 'Back to Mom and Pop. They haven't seen Sidonia.'

'But there's work here,' countered Percy.

He was keenly aware that Canada, especially out here in Alberta, was a young and growing country. As venturers pushed ever further into remoter territory there was a guarantee of plentiful work for tradesmen such as carpenters, and especially for those prepared to tolerate the pioneering lifestyle.

But Dolly prevailed, as she did throughout their fractured time together. Dolly had a will of her own and, as a neighbour was latter to describe her, was 'a woman of questionable character … who refused to accept the responsibility of home life'.

Together with Victor, Sidonia and Percy she returned to Minnesota in time to give birth to Douglas F Nicholas on Boxing Day 1916.

From then on, Percy Nicholas, the Cornish son of a serpentine cutter's daughter and a keeper of the Lizard lighthouse, made his life among the communities settled around Minnesota's multitude of lakes. My Celtic roots had again crossed the Atlantic, although this time to flounder rather than to flourish in the fertile lands of rural north-eastern America.

Dolly went on to have eight children, but four of them, including first-born Victor, were illegitimate. There was, however, a lengthy gap between the birth of Douglas in 1915 and the arrival of Valleere (also recorded as Valerie) in 1921 which, in view of the large families usual in those pre-Pill days, suggests she may have suffered a run of stillborn and infant deaths similar to those experienced by Percy's mother.

Percy's only absence during this period was during the final stages of the First World War when he belatedly answered the call to arms and went to the recruiting office in Minneapolis on 18 June 1918 to enlist in the Canadian Overseas Expeditionary Force.

He returned from Europe unscathed into Toronto on the *Mauretania* and when he crossed back into the States he told the US Border Force he intended taking out American citizenship, although this was not compulsory. Naturalisation was a two-step process and by the time of the 1930 census Percy had obtained his 'first papers' by filing a declaration of intent to become a US citizen. Ten years later, however, he had progressed no further and was still noted as 'having first papers'. Once again, the picture is of a man who told the authorities what they wanted to know rather than state the reality of the situation.

His most pressing need was to remain employed. At various times Percy is officially described as a carpenter, a bridge carpenter, a house carpenter and, for a while, as a painter. He chased work and adapted his basic skills to suit employers' needs.

These were the turbulent years of the Depression and Prohibition, with high unemployment, rampant poverty and poor living conditions for the millions of have-nots. Like many other struggling families, the Nicholas brood did it tough, a situation not helped by the death on 1 December 1926 of son Douglas at the age of 10, nor by the arrival of son Thomas on 8 March 1927.

Life for the Nicholas family then plummeted quicker than a broken lift-shaft.

By the time of the 1930 US census, which coincided with the death of his father, lighthouse-keeper Charles Edwin Nicholas back in England, Percy was living in rented accommodation at 1702, 6th Street North, Hennepin County, Minneapolis, with no trace anywhere of Dolly. Sharing the house with him were children Sidonia, Valleere, Gerald and Audrey, plus eldest son Victor and his wife Beulah.

There is no mention of youngest son Thomas. However, precisely nine months later, Dolly gives birth to daughter Patricia Ann, an event likely responsible for her disappearance and leading to a separation from Percy that began in 1925 and lasted for several years.

She probably took youngest son Thomas with her, an unfortunate move for him as he became an inmate of the Catholic Asylum for Boys in Minneapolis before he reached his teens and eventually died from an overdose, unmarried and living in San Francisco, on 1 December 1985.

Throughout the 1930s, Dolly and Patricia frequently changed address – sometimes renting a place of their own, sometimes reduced to 'rooming' but they were never far from Percy or the rest of the family.

Victor, a shipper of paint and glass in one document but really flitting from one short-term job to another, and Beulah found their own place to live, also nearby.

But they were having troubles of their own, not helped by theirs being a marriage 'forced' upon them, according to a statement made by Victor to prison authorities, by Beulah's staunch Lutheran family when her pregnancy could no longer be disguised.

Victor spent much of the 1930s and early 1940s first as an inmate of the St Cloud Reformatory and then the Minnesota State Prison. He had been sentenced on 26 October 1932 for second degree assault during a robbery at a service station, an offence of which he always protested he was innocent. He later committed conspiracy to defraud the state's emergency relief fund.

This was too much for Beulah; she remained loyal to him for much of his time in gaol but eventually filed for divorce and married Harold August Schoeben from the tight-knit Scandinavian Lutheran community of her parents.

It was not until the early 1940s that Victor finally emerged from the reformatory and the state prison and on 2 December 1967 he mar-

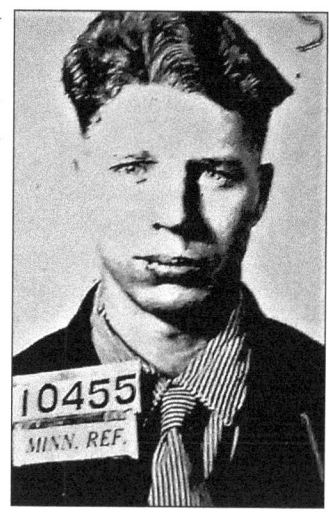

Victor Nicholas mug shot
[picture: Minnesota Historical Society archives]

ried Charlene Joyce Tompkins in Minneapolis. But it was a short-lived relationship; on 13 February 1972 he died from heart disease.

Earlier, younger brother John had answered the call to arms and on 29 September 1942 left his life as an attendant on filling stations and parking lots to enlist at Fort Snelling, Minneapolis, as a private in the US Air Corps 'for the duration of the War or other emergency, plus six months, subject to the discretion of the President or otherwise according to law'.

How he fared and where during the conflict is among the stories yet to be uncovered.

Victor and Dolly were reunited when he fell ill in the early 1940s. She took on the role of nurse and carer until his death on 8 July 1944. Dolly followed him less than two years later, on 21 March 1946. Both are buried in Crystal Lake Cemetery, Minneapolis.

It is because of Cornish cousin Percy Nicholas and his family that the Berrys' Celtic roots are settled deep into the Minnesota landscape. But it is a dark and tangled growth as any hopes Percy harboured of achieving success and prosperity fell well short of the mark.

Lured by curiosity, I later tumbled into that deep dark pit that awaits all family historians who venture too far out along the more fragile branches of their trees. Here, built around the misdeeds of son Victor, I found the full story of Percy's American misadventure.

And it is a very sad tale indeed ....

NO GET OUT OF JAIL CARD FOR VICTOR

VICTOR WILBUR NICHOLAS ALREADY had a criminal record under the alias of Jack Nichols when he appeared before Judge A W Selover on 3 March 1933 on a charge of armed robbery. As prosecuting county attorney L J Gleason revealed, Victor (or Jack Nichols, as he claimed his name to be) had been arrested in Minneapolis in 1927 for disorderly conduct and given a suspended workhouse sentence. A charge of reckless driving in 1931 was dismissed but he then served twenty-six months for second degree assault.

Although Victor claimed he was completely innocent, the jury decided to convict him and he was sentenced to a term of five to twenty years in St Cloud State Reformatory for Men.

According to his plea, Victor was an innocent bystander when police arrested him on 2 February 1933:

> I stopped in at the Franklin Cooperative Creamery's main plant to inquire about securing work. A fellow told me to go to the branch plant at 26th and East Franklin Avenue and I started walking. About 5.30pm I was in the vicinity of East Franklin and Cedar Avenue and I walked into a Tankar gas station for the purpose of using the washroom.
>
> As I stepped into the door a police car drove in and two men in the gas station yelled 'cops' and jumped out through a rear window. The police began shooting so I also jumped out the window but stopped to avoid being shot. I was convicted by a jury of attempting to rob this filling station.
>
> **From St Cloud State Reformatory records**

When asked the reason for his crime on his admission to the reformatory on 6 March 1933, he again stated: 'I am innocent'.

The mug shot attached to his personal file shows a good-looking, freckled and tousle-haired young man, neat in attire and appearance. He stood 5ft 10.5in tall and weighed 10st 4lb (64kg) but was described as sallow and thirty-five pounds underweight for his large build.

His IQ was assessed as 107, having reached seventh grade in junior high school. He left home at age fifteen because, in his own words, 'family broke up' and parents 'couldn't get along' and the overall atmosphere was 'not so good'.

On prison documents, he describes his marriage to Beulah Kuehl as 'forced', which seems possible as she gave birth to the first of their three children six months after their marriage before a Justice of the Peace. Others have told me it was a willing union but have no proof of it being so. However, Victor did state their conjugal relations were 'good' and he supported his family with income from a succession of short-term jobs – the longest, five months working for an upholsterer.

Character assessments from prison officers painted a portrait of light and dark. Some saw him as efficient, conscientious, alert and trustworthy during periods when he was a trusty overseeing, and even teaching, various vocational activities in the prison. Others claimed he was 'untruthful, insists he is not guilty' and had incurred reports and penalties for 'gambling, being noisy, talking, and smoking without permission', which hardly seem like hard core infractions.

On 21 April 1934 Victor sought an interview with the warden, H W Whittier, at which he stated:

> *I am serving two consecutive sentences of five and twenty years respectively. I have just been to the board and received a continuance for one year on the first sentence. As I interpret the rules governing the board as the rules stated in my rule book, I could not receive more than nine months. I think perhaps if you will grant me an interview you can put me straight concerning them. Respectfully yours, Victor Nicholas.*

On 17 April 1935, and following more similar appeals, Victor was discharged by the State Parole Board of Minnesota and ordered to begin immediately serving his second sentence of five to 20 years for the first and prior conviction for attempted armed robbery. This was due to expire on 12 March 1948. However, the board also considered Victor's numerous appeals and protests and commuted his sentence to a maximum of six years 'on condition he lead a law-abiding life'.

On 21 February 1938, this was further commuted to three years and nine months, expiring on 5 March 1938.

While serving this lesser sentence Victor was reported seven times for misconduct, once being placed in solitary confinement for involvement as editor of the in-house journal, *The Pillar*, when it urged inmates to strike. 'This is unfair,' he protested.

He maintained he had never asked to work on *The Pillar* and had been promised a transfer that never eventuated. Solitary confinement hit him hard.

'*This is getting me down,*' he wrote to Warden Whittier on 5 June 1936. '*I've kept my balance this long by plenty of work both in and out of my cell but now I find myself with 21 hours in my cell with nothing to do. I am fully aware I am here for punishment, but I can't see the benefit either to the state or myself in my being persecuted and I am inclined to believe this is nothing less than that. I am either on my way to court or locked in my cell. Another month of this and I'll be on my way to St Peter. Maybe that is self-pity. If so, that is a step in that direction already.*'

Despite being punished for his work on *The Pillar*, he still pleaded to go back there. '*If not, some kind of work outside would be appreciated.*'

During this first spell at the reformatory, Victor studied and worked as a bookkeeper, even taking on a teaching role for a while, and spent five months at the reformatory's penal camp at Moose Lake, working mostly as a carpenter and a stone-cutter, for a while acting as foreman. The chances of rehabilitation and a return to a law-abiding life looked promising.

His release on 5 March 1938 was his big chance to return to society; he even had his citizenship status restored within two weeks of his release. All he had to do was stay out of trouble and keep to the terms of his parole.

But he blew it.

On 2 December 1939, Victor stood before Judge Matthew Joyce and a jury in the US Federal Court in Minneapolis. He was one of twenty-five

defendants charged with conspiracy to violate the Emergency Relief Act set up to support disadvantaged families, such as his own. They were accused of using force and threats to prevent fellow workers receiving payments due to them under the terms of the Act.

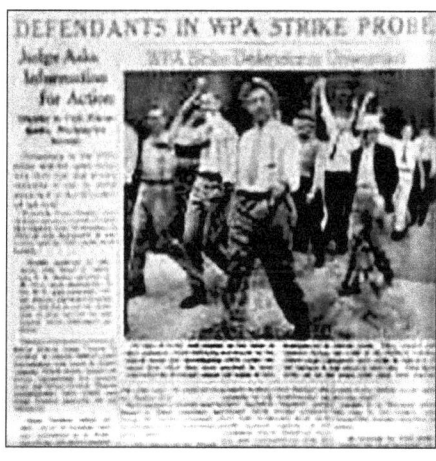

All were found guilty. For Victor, this meant he had violated the terms of his parole and incurred the restitution of his original sentence of five to twenty years. It also brought him into the clutches of the Federal Court system and a transfer on 1 May 1940 from the reformatory to the Federal Correctional Institution (Minnesota State Prison) in Sandstone, Minnesota. With adjustments for good and bad conduct his earliest possible release date was 5 June 1941, but neither wife Beulah nor

Victor Nicholas makes the news with the protest march

mistress Mae Erkilla were prepared to wait that long.

In one last desperate attempt at freedom and a reversal of the injustice he believed he had suffered, Victor sought Presidential clemency. On 27 May 1940, he was told this had been denied.

It all added up to a long time behind bars for cousin Victor, whether under his earlier alias of Nichols or his true name of Nicholas. At least he had company: his uncle, Lewis Runyon, and cousin, Ralph Runyon, were both serving time for first degree robbery.

In the early days of his confinement, Victor made several pleas to have his sentence reduced and obtain some sort of support for Beulah and their family.

Beulah was living in four rooms on the second floor of 2018 4th Street North, Minneapolis, close to the railyards and the city's once thriving warehouse district but now in rapid decline. She and her three small children were dependant on the Board of Public Relief to pay for groceries, fuel and their $12 a month rent. They had only a few pieces of furniture, no money in the bank and an outstanding doctor's bill of $27. She had applied for mother's aid, but her case would not be heard for several months.

Not that things were much better before Victor was sent to gaol. Although he had tried to support her and the children, Beulah said this only occurred when he was working – and he had been out of work for the past year. None of her own family were able to support them and Victor's parents, Percy and Dolly, were separated and living off public welfare.

In an initial report to the parole board, parole agent Miss B M Mold wrote that:

'The wife [Beulah] *appears to be very fond of inmate and expects to re-establish her home with him upon his release. She claims bad company, idleness and anxiety over family were the causes of commission of crime.'*

Beulah told her Victor underwent an appendectomy in January 1932 and had been out of work for a year before his arrest. Earlier, he had sold radios on commission, worked four months operating a steam press and spent a similar period driving a truck for the Johnson Fish Company. She confirmed she had been pregnant by Victor when her parents forced them to marry.

All in all, a sad and gloomy state of affairs with little hope of improvement. Yet for all Victor's failings, Miss Mold considered him *'kind and considerate of his family and interested in his children'*.

Her recommendation of an allowance of $6 a month to support the family, the cheque to go directly to Beulah, was approved on 28 June 1933. For Beulah, this was not enough:

'I have been informed I should be receiving more,' she wrote to the board on 9 August. *'Perhaps there has been a mistake. I have three children and all the help I receive is city relief, which is very little. I applied for a pension nearly six months ago but as yet have received nothing. Will you please see if there has been a misunderstanding and inform me to that effect?'*

Miss Mold made further enquiries and reported the family was *'getting along nicely'*. Beulah and the children had moved to 1702 6th Street North, Minneapolis, where *'the children are well and appear to be receiving good care'*.

The state was paying their rent and had increased its fortnightly grocery order to $9. Miss Mold said Beulah's application for mother's aid was still pending and her case would be reviewed when aid had been approved. She saw no reason for any additional help.

Beulah clearly did not agree.

On 11 December 1933, she pleaded with the board to reconsider and shorten his sentence because '*it is his first offence and the jury recommended leniency, but I cannot see that he got it*'.

Despite evidence to the contrary, she alleged that although she had applied for aid she had '*not as yet received a penny. We are destitutely in need of everything. We are all alone and I have been trying to struggle on in an up-righteous way, but everything is against me*'.

Later that month, Miss Mold told the parole board the family's budget had been worked out at a very precise $50.86 a month, of which one third ($16.95) had been referred to the state. She added, '*This young mother appears quite capable and is interested in her family. She comes from better stock than the inmate* [cousin Victor], *whose family background is poor*'.

She recommended state aid, which included Victor's earnings, be increased to $12 a month. The board eventually approved this and back-dated payment to 1 January 1934.

Credit must go to the parole board for the prompt and diligent – even caring – way it made sure Victor's family received all the support due to them. As soon as he was admitted to the reformatory it wasted no time in examining their circumstances and anything that might justify his plea for parole. As a letter sent on 23 June 1933 to Victor's family, employers and associates explained:

> '*We commence investigation in all cases while the facts are still fresh. An early letter from you stating the nature of your contacts with him and what you know of his past life, his habits and work records, the character of his associates and is general attitude towards society will be of great assistance.*'

The response was mixed from the fourteen people contacted and, in some cases, was non-existent. The Park Transfer Company, where Victor claimed he had worked, had no recollection of him. A Joseph Burger said he had only heard of him second hand since the attempted robbery.

However, although Victor had worked for A S Johnson Fish Company only for a brief time as an extra truck driver, '*his services were satisfactory as he worked steady and seemed quite conscientious ... he seemed to be cheerful and pleasant and did not have any trouble getting along with the other workmen employed by us*'.

Stella Vasey, a Minneapolis club organiser and former neighbour, wrote that Victor's father, my Cornish cousin Percy Nicholas, was *'a hard-working man of very little education ... who did his best to bring up a good, honest, American family'.* She noted that he was *'only a stepfather',* but had married Victor's mother, Dolly, when Victor was very young, bringing Victor up as his own son.

Vasey was damning in her opinion of Dolly:

> *'The mother neglected her children and was a woman of questionable character. I knew this woman as a common law wife and mother who refused to accept the responsibility of home life. The father did his best but was not quite as enforcing as he should have been, so we might say the home environment of Victor Nicholas was not of the best'.*

She recalled that,

'Victor himself played with my son, has slept in my house and has eaten at my table. The boy was a common freckled face American boy, mischievous perhaps but not rowdy or, in slang, hard boiled. His education because of his parents was neglected. He did not work after he left school. In the fall he would go to the harvest fields and work on the farm. He liked to play ball, swim and fish just like any other boy'.

However, in Vasey's opinion: *'I think Victor must realise that crime does not pay and that he must think of his wife and babies'.*

Nor did Dolly do much to help her son. The rambling, semi-literate and poorly punctuated letter she wrote to the board on 6 July 1933 would have likely done his case more harm than good. It did not help that an earlier attempt by Victor to write to her had gone astray because she had moved house and not told him of her new address:

'I am only glad as I can to cooperate with your people in his behalf as to his past life he was always a very good son work always when he could and was always glad to share his money and home as long as he was home, and was always good to his little family as long as he could get work to do it with. I think you could (get) that information from his employers and as to his friend he had some very nice boys from a youngster up and he always brought his friends home and I met they all were very nice young men and he always took interest in good clean ....'

Beulah's carpenter father, William, hid any disappointment he must have felt with his son-in-law. Victor had worked for him at various times in his early relationship with Beulah and, *'has always been a good worker. In all his time here [Veblen, Beulah's home town] I have always found him honest and true. I do not know anything about his habits since he went to Minneapolis but during the several years he has been around here he has showed himself a Gentlemn [sic] and I have never heard anyone say anything bad about him. It was a grate surprice [sic] to hear of his case'.*

To Frank Williams, who said he had known him for many years, Victor was *'just an average boy'* and *'at heart, not bad'*.

None of this persuaded the parole board to reduce his sentence or reconsider his case.

Maybe it was a desperate plea on his behalf from Beulah that did the trick. After visiting Victor in prison, she wrote to warden Whittier on 1 March 1938 from 326 25th Ave North, Minneapolis, querying a possible early release thanks to thirty days' good behaviour time Victor had told her he had earned.

'I don't understand much about it but that you can ask for it for him. It would make the children and I very happy and him tho if you would do this. Mr Erwin of the parole board still maintains it was their intention that he be released at once but evidently the papers were made out differently. It was a big disappointment to us because our son 8 years old has been in the hospital three weeks. I promised him his father would be home when he was well enough to come home. So if you can, Mr Whittier, get for him that time it will bring him that much closer to us.'

Four days later, on 5 March 1938, Victor was released. And soon proved to be his own worst enemy …

Despite his frequent claims of innocence and injustice, Victor was easily drawn into bad company and this time he excelled himself.

He became embroiled in a violent mass conspiracy to defraud Minnesota's emergency relief fund, set up to support destitute families such as his own. This flagrant breach of the parole conditions for his newfound freedom, saw the authorities moving quickly to reinstate his original sentence even before he appeared in court on this latest charge.

For a while, he remained free on bond while his background and behaviour were again investigated. None appeared positive. The reformatory reported an odd mix of insubordination and rule-breaking alongside spasmodic attempts at self-improvement. Other documents revealed the breakdown of his marriage.

Victor and Beulah's record of marriage

Beulah eventually accepted Victor was a lost cause and unlikely to provide the support she and her young family desperately needed. As Victor explained in a letter to warden Whittier, on 4 April 1940:

'My wife and I have not lived together since last July and she is divorcing me to marry another man'.

This letter confirmed Victor had launched into a new relationship with Mae Erkilla, a woman the authorities unflatteringly described as his 'moll'. To them, it came as no surprise. Since Victor's return to prison in January, Mae had sent a succession of letters proclaiming her undying love and devotion and that *I'll wait for ever for you.*

She told him of efforts to get lawyers to take an interest in his case, sent him birthday wishes, wrote of the agony his absence was causing her, and revealed that she had formed a close association with his mother and other family members.

Mae the moll had stepped into Beulah's shoes.

For several months, none of this reached Victor. The warden informed Mae that, *'inasmuch as Victor Nicholas is still legally married you will not be given permission to correspond and visit him'.*

Victor's mother, the now ailing Dolly, received similar notice, but for a different reason:

> *When Victor Nicholas was returned here he was placed in third grade for a period of thirty days. He will receive his grade on February 5th and you may write to him after that date, and also visit if you wish. While in third grade he cannot write and receive mail.*

This was in response to a letter [one of several] Dolly wrote to warden Whittier asking when she could see him and if he had received his mail and clothing,

> 'as I been writing and I didn't receive any letter in return. I didn't know when I could see him and when I can write as I am his mother and I am the one to receive his letters'.

Victor also protested against the withholding of his mail and in seeking permission to write to Mae Erkilla revealed, *my mother is entirely dependent on her for help and friendship and she is also my girlfriend.*

As Beulah was planning to remarry, he saw no reason *'why my morals should be questioned concerning a matter of censored correspondence'.*

He claimed his lawyer had written to him a couple of times, but he had received neither letter and could see no reason they should be withheld. He asked to have them.

As for visits from his mother and Mae,

> 'if I am to be permitted any visits; my mother could not come alone and I don't know anyone else who could or would come with her. These requests are necessary to my mother's wellbeing and damned convenient to mine'.

Comments made by Mae in her several letters to Victor showed she was not only besotted by him but had been closely involved in activities surrounding the conspiracy to defraud the benefits system.

It was during this period of fractured communication, by mail and in person, that Mae wrote some of her most heartfelt letters, spilling out her love and devotion.

On 14 January 1940, the occasion of Victor's birthday, she wrote wishing him all the happiness in the world but said to wish him Happy Birthday would just be a mockery.

> 'I know my dear you aren't happy. I'm not either. So lonesome for you sweetheart it doesn't seem like anything can be crueller than this separation. I didn't think I had it in me to love any man as I love you. It would have been better if I didn't, but it is too late now and while I am so unhappy I am also glad I love you and

maybe it won't be so long before I can have you back. … every minute and hr of the day and night my thoughts are with you and I dream of you every nite. Oh! if only I could see that curly head again, is this monotonous? I can't help it I Love you so very much and I need you dear'.

She was sending him slippers for his birthday along with a box containing his underwear, socks, hankies and razor blades and shaving brush.

She hoped he received them but that may have been a forlorn wish judging by the way he was being deprived of letters and visitors. She sent him a birthday card although she had no idea if he would receive it. At this stage of their relationship, Victor was very much her man and she was fighting all the way on his behalf.

However, she did his cause little good by accompanying Victor's lawyer, Vance Skahan, on a prison visit and pretending to be Victor's fourteen-year-old sister, Vallerie.

The ruse was quickly detected and, as warden Whittier informed Mr Skahan and reported to the parole board, this form of deception did nothing to improve Victor's standing.

Mae's association with the lawyer indicated her determination to clear Victor's name and achieve his release. Her letters made frequent reference to meetings with lawyers and to incidents around the alleged conspiracy.

Vance Skahen told her although it was like butting his head against a stone wall, he thought there was a loophole and he would find it. Mae said an Ed Palmquest was the only one sticking by him but the rest were fair weather friends. '*It is the truth and you may as well know it. Ed said he'd get busy and see if there wasn't some way to get you out*'.

Vance Skahan told her he felt exhausted not because he had worked so hard but because he felt that he had not accomplished anything. But he assured her he would not give up until something happened one way or the other.

Mae gave a faint but intriguing clue about the conspiracy in telling Victor on 4 January,

'there was a piece on the front page yesterday about that Hastings deal, even told about the door'.

On 12 January she tells him that when she had stopped at his sister Vallerie's place on the way to see his mother,

> *'I had to talk fast over there. They blame you for being mixed up in this, but I guess I told them ... there couldn't possibly have been any other way under the circumstances.*

Again, she suggests Victor has been unfairly treated:

'How I wish you had never gone to your mother's that day, but perhaps it would have been the same thing. That Hastings deal was certainly the result of this'.

Everything began to take its toll. Mae was so sick for two days that she couldn't get out of bed except to crawl to a phone and call the lawyers. *'Dizzy and weak but I am better today. I was afraid I was headed for a nervous breakdown or the nut house, that wouldn't be so good'.*

Although found guilty on 4 December 1939, Victor, his co-conspirators Ralph Core and Charles Grider (alias Jack Bailey) and twenty-two others had to wait for pre-sentence investigations to be completed before appearing for sentence in the US District Court on 24 March 1940.

By then, it had been decided that rather than face additional jail time Victor should now serve the full term of his original five to 20 years with all commutations cancelled. A bureaucratic battle ensued over whether he should remain at the State Reformatory for Men or be confined in the Minnesota State Prison at Stillwater as his most recent crime had been a federal offence.

For a while, the reformatory continued to enjoy the pleasure of his company. Eventually, however, he was sent to Stillwater to complete his original sentence. He was still there in March 1943 when the prison started planning an activities program for him.

On 8 April, while still at the reformatory, he received permission to correspond with Mae Erkilla and for Mae to visit him *'for your mother's sake'*.

Mae – listed as 'friend' – visited him on the afternoon of 19 April, which is the last mention of her so far found in any available records. The assumption is that unrequited passion for her tousled-haired lover withered in the face of his long-term incarceration.

When he was eventually released, which his daughter Donna told me was in 1942, he enrolled in the AA, found gainful employment and became a good father to his seven children.

At least until 1961 when he separated from his wife, was arrested and jailed for a wholefood store robbery in Wisconsin and his daughter cut off all connections.

On 2 December 1967 he married Charlene Tompkins in Hennepin, Minneapolis. Sadly this became a short-lived union as he died on 13 February 1972 after undergoing open-heart surgery. He was buried as a US Army Veteran with honour guard in Fort Snelling Cemetery, South Minneapolis on 2 May 1973.

CORNISHMEN GOING FOR GOLD

CONNECTIONS TO MY CORNISH cousins took a fresh twist when I discovered one family of Joses had put down their roots in the Australian state of Victoria, little more than an hour's drive from where I had made my home for more than forty years. Their remains lie in the same former gold rush region where my daughter until recently ran a country pub that has little changed since being built in those turbulent gold rush times.

The patriarch of this adventurous offshoot was Richard Jose, born in the Lizard Peninsula fishing village of Mullion in 1821 and a great-uncle of my cousin and lighthouse-keeper's wife, Mary Ann Sidonia Jose.

He was also the brother of those two ne'er-do-wells, Stephen and James, the sheep-stealers and general thieves, the former having drowned when fleeing the law and the latter deported for life for his crimes.

Early exploration of Richard's story indicated enough raw material to weave an entire book – probably a novel, as so much of it seems steeped more in fantasy than fact and especially as it is set in times long before international travel became measured in hours or days rather than weeks and months.

The usual reliable sources show that in 1841 he was a farmer at Little Trethveas at Landewednack, on the Lizard Peninsular. In October that year, and still only twenty, he married Matilda Jago Cocking (or Cockling) from Wendron.

The first surprise comes two years later when they registered the birth of daughter Jane Jose in, of all places, Quebec, Canada. To date, no record has been found of how or when the couple made their transatlantic voyage, nor of the equally surprising return trip which, less than two years later, brought them back to Little Trethveas where a second daughter, Christina Jago Jose, was born in 1845.

In all subsequent records the intriguing fact remains constant, and unexplained: that Jane Jose was born in Quebec during her parents' two-year absence from the Lizard.

Maybe Richard, like many before him and since, had thought there were better opportunities in Canada but was disappointed by what he found. The reason for their move to Quebec could be a family dispute over their relationship, even a child conceived out of wedlock. Perhaps Matilda was the trigger for their return to Landewednack. She would have felt acutely homesick, which would have been worsened by having a baby at her breast that none of her family were likely to see.

And so they returned to face whatever music awaited.

Richard resumed work first as a labourer and then as a farmer, doing well enough to be recorded in the 1851 census as having fifty acres at Little Trethveas. By then, their family had increased with the births of Elizabeth, Emily and James Henry.

But, for Richard, the lure of a new life overseas persisted.

'We can do better than this,' he insisted.

'Better than Canada?' said Matilda, her voice full of doubt. 'It will have to be.'

She was far from convinced by her husband's enthusiasm for making a fresh start in faraway Australia. The thought of the long, arduous journey was enough to add further stress to a mind and body already strained by motherhood and the daily struggle of life on the Lizard. To go all that way seemed more like the sentence handed down to her brother-in-law, James Jose, deported and gaoled for life.

'If James can make a success of it, so can we,' said Richard, as if tuning in to her thoughts. He was referring to brief letters home from his brother in Australia. 'He got a pardon, married a free woman and is making a go of things.'

'Of course he'd say he's doing well,' sniped Matilda. 'Always protesting his innocence, that one.'

Richard shrugged. 'That's as maybe, but you have to see there's opportunities we don't have here.'

And so it was that Richard, Matilda and their five children paid £12 and joined the convict ship *Neptune* as assisted migrants on its voyage from Ireland to Australia. The ship had sailed from Cork on 26 October 1843, under the command of William Ferris, with 308 bounty emigrants aboard. On arrival in Sydney on 11 February 1844 she was placed in quarantine for three days because of an outbreak of smallpox. Ten people died during the voyage, among them the Joses' year-old daughter Elizabeth.

By arriving in Sydney, Richard had the chance to reunite with his brother James, now a freeman and living with his wife Jane (Curtis), also a former convict.

And now – at least until further information comes to light – Richard's story becomes wrapped in mystery. Several facts emerge:

1. Sometime over the next few years he and Matilda return to England as he next appears as departing Liverpool on 30 December 1857 on a 140-day voyage bringing him back to Australia.

2. Matilda remains in England, dying in Bodmin Lunatic Asylum in 1873 from a catatonic seizure.

3. Accompanying Richard on his return to Australia is Charlotte 'Jose', who is later revealed to be Charlotte Yendell (or Yendall), born on the Lizard Peninsula in 1827 at Ruan Minor.

4. They arrive not in Sydney but in Melbourne where Richard describes himself as a miner, not the farm labourer and groom of earlier times.

5. Between 1859 and 1865, Richard fathers four more children with 'wife' Charlotte while living in the outer suburbs of Melbourne at Epsom and Hawthorn rather than in any of the recognised goldmining areas of the time.

6. On 16 March 1889 (well after the death of Matilda in the Bodmin Asylum) Richard marries Charlotte at St Paul's Church, Sandhurst, deep in the state of Victoria's goldmining region, thus bringing legitimacy to what had clearly been an almost lifelong relationship.

It was in Sandhurst (which reverted to its original and current name of Bendigo in 1891) that Richard – described by one who knew him as 'a big large man who settled at Antimony Creek' - gained a certain amount of fame as a wrestler at the many Cornish wrestling matches held throughout the state. It was also where the couple remained for the rest of their days, raising their children and establishing yet another foreign outpost of the Joses of Landewednack, none of who returned to Cornwall.

There were others who never returned for far sadder reasons … and more of them later.

Meanwhile, back in Sandhurst, there was another Jose newly arrived from the Lizard Peninsula. This was Mary, born in St Keverne in November 1829 to Francis and Mary Jose and now married to labourer Richard Stephens who somehow persuaded her to forsake family and friends in order to achieve a far better life on the goldfields of Victoria.

So determined was he to achieve this dream that Richard scratched together the fare for the arduous voyage with more than two hundred other hopefuls, many of them assisted passage migrants, on board the 765-tonne barque *Fairlie*.

He, Mary and daughters Christina Jane and Philippa Sidonia (there's that name again) sailed from Plymouth in the summer of 1856 and arrived in Melbourne on 4 June. And there's every likelihood there was at least one familiar face waiting on the quayside to greet them, given the number of Lizard inhabitants who had decided Australia was the place to be.

They went on to have five more daughters and two sons (one surviving for less than a year), eventually settling in Heathcote and never returning to the Lizard with Richard dying aged 57 in 1887 and Mary following him two years later at the age 60.

THE MEN WHO WENT TO WAR

THROUGHOUT YEARS OF BEING a bystander at Armistice Day commemorations and the solemn ceremonies of Anzac Day it seemed unbelievable that I had no connection to the many who had fallen in the wars of the twentieth century. The closest association with military men was my father's staunch membership of 'Dad's Army' – the Home Guard – during our World War II sojourn in the then thriving Lancashire fishing port of Fleetwood. He proudly rose to the rank of lieutenant, polished his boots and buckles to a mirror shine before each weekly parade and kept his rifle ever ready to fight the Hun.

Apart from this display of home front bravado, my Celtic kinfolk seemed to deny the oft-repeated statement that no family was left untouched by the twentieth century's great conflicts. The more I thought about it, the more it seemed unlikely, almost a denial of the undeniable. Yet there had never been the slightest whisper of a relative who had failed to return. My ancestors appeared to have missed war service by reason of age or because many plied skilled trades in HM Dockyards and were thus exempt.

But all that changed when I delved into the foliage of the family tree. Death certificates yielded clues and pointed the way into military records and the tragic and sudden end to several young lives. I now know for sure that at least three ancestors died in that heinous conflict, two leaving no remains.

One Welsh cousin saw her four sons go to war; one was blown to pieces, two returned but died early from gassing and other injuries, and only one lived on to experience old age.

Other Celtic kinsmen survived but continued to endure the results of injury and sickness incurred on the battlefront. Old age was mostly not theirs to enjoy.

When Cornish cousin Richard Henry Jose signed on the dotted line at the Royal Navy recruitment base in Devonport on 28 March 1908 he was exactly eighteen years old and committing to serve the nation for the next twelve years.

Like all seamen recruits, the 5ft 9in former stoneworker, with brown hair, hazel eyes and fresh complexion, was posted to HMS *Impregnable,* a training ship based at Devonport. She was a former 121-gun ship built in 1860, originally named HMS *Howe,* then renamed HMS *Bulwark* until 1886, when she became the *Impregnable.*

In the early days of his enlistment, Richard carried the basic rank of 'boy' and endured the tough routine all the services mete out to new recruits. Initial training was based on a rough and ready system that still had a big hangover from sailing days when the only way to learn was by doing every task again and again. There was little need for classroom theory. Working and living conditions were harsh and unforgiving.

Further training followed on HMS *Hogue,* named after the 1692 Battle of La Hogue and launched in Barrow-in-Furness on 13 August 1900. After fitting out in Plymouth, she was assigned to the Channel Fleet in November 1902.

On 11 March 1904 she collided with the merchant ship SS *Meurthe* and returned to port for a refit before transferring to the China station.

Two years later she became the boys' training ship for the 4th Cruiser Squadron on the North America and West Indies Station. By the time Richard enlisted she had been reduced to reserve status at Devonport and, within months, assigned to the reserve Third Fleet at the Nore.

The *Hogue* was moved on, and so was Richard – to his first 'real' ship, the battleship HMS *Majestic,* one of the most modern and best-equipped fighting vessels of that time. He now had the rank of ordinary seaman but within months was promoted to able seaman and posted to the battleship HMS *Ocean.*

After seeing service in China and suffering damage in a typhoon, the *Ocean* had undergone several refits and was now recommissioned for duty with the Mediterranean Fleet, giving Richard his first seagoing experience. Soon, however, the *Ocean* was back in Devonport, transferred to the new Home Fleet and scheduled for yet another refit as an anxious Admiralty started making sure its ships were war-ready.

For Richard, this meant a further shore-based stint at HMS *Vivid* before being posted to the heavily armed cruiser, HMS *Diana,* where he remained until April 1913. Then came another shore posting at HMS *Vivid* as he took the next step up the ranks – to leading seaman.

As a nervy Europe began ramping up preparations for war, Richard and his fellow sailors began to sense the realities of what lay ahead. No more training and rehearsals; no more mock battles. Soon, if all the predictions were correct, they would be fighting for survival – of themselves, their ships and the nation.

On 1 July 1913 Richard stepped aboard the armoured cruiser HMS *Warrior,* recently transferred to the 1st Cruiser Squadron of the Mediterranean Fleet and began what was to become the fateful final three years of his young life.

The *Warrior*, ordered as part of the 1903-04 naval construction programme, had been laid down on 5 November 1903 at Pembroke Dockyard, thus providing another link between my Welsh and Cornish Celtic ancestors.

With the outbreak of World War I, Richard was soon in the thick of things.

Immediately hostilities began, *Warrior* was involved in the pursuit of the German battlecruiser *Goeben* and light cruiser *Breslau,* but was ordered not to engage them due to the Breslau's more powerful guns, heavier armour and faster speed. Within days, the *Warrior* became part of the Allied sweep that led to the sinking of the Austro-Hungarian light cruiser SMS *Zenta* during the Battle of Antivari in August 1914.

A few days later she was ordered to Suez to defend the canal against Turkish attacks and remained there until 6 November when she was called to Gibraltar to join a squadron of French and British ships to search for German warships still at sea off the African coast.

The following month, *Warrior* joined the Grand Fleet and was assigned to the 1st Cruiser Squadron under Rear Admiral Sir Robert Keith Arbuthnot, major players in what was to become the most disastrous sea battle of all time at Jutland in May 1916.

Richard remained with the *Warrior* until transferring to the squadron flagship, the armoured cruiser HMS *Defence* – another Pembroke-built ship – on 25 April 1915. Here he continued his steady move up the ranks with promotion to petty officer in recognition of a career performance that had been consistently assessed as 'very good'.

It was a move that made all the difference between life and death for the former stonemason from Landewednack.

Although Richard's former ship, the *Warrior*, eventually sank from battle damage during the Battle of Jutland, 743 of its crew survived. In the same bombardment, the *Defence* sank with all hands, Richard among them.

HMS Defiance: ready for action at Jutland in 1916

Rear Admiral Arbuthnot later said *Defence* should never have been part of the British battle line; an old armoured cruiser not built for such actions. Rather her role was as an armed ship that could interdict an adversary's merchant shipping at sea.

A design flaw had resulted in great bins, capable of holding between 40-60 cordite bags, being built in the midships area between the main fore and aft 9.2inch Mk XI guns and where there were ten secondary 7.5-inch guns, five on each wing, supplied with shells and cordite from the main magazines.

During the battle, *Warrior* and *Defence* had closed in to engage the disabled German light cruiser SMS *Wiesbaden*. When within 5500 yards of the *Wiesbaden* they were seen by the German battlecruiser SMS *Derfflinger* and four nearby battleships. Under heavy gunfire from the German ships, *Defence* was hit by two salvos that caused the aft 9.2-inch magazine to explode. The resulting fire spread via the ammunition passages to detonate the adjacent 7.5-inch magazines. The ship exploded with the loss of all on board, between 893 and 903 men.

St Wynwallow Church war memorial bears the name of Richard Jose

Richard's name appears on the war memorial in St Wynwallow Church, Church Cove, Landewednack, and on the Plymouth Naval Memorial. The official record states, *Killed in Action, body not recovered for burial.*

** It was believed that the *Defence* had been reduced to fragments by the explosion, but the wreck was discovered in mid-1984 by Clive Cussler and marine surveyors. In 2001, a dive team led by nautical archaeologist Innes McCartney found her to be largely intact. Along with other Jutland wrecks, the *Defence* is now a protected place under the Protection of Military Remains Act 1986, to discourage further damage to this resting place of approximately 900 men.

A relative by marriage of the unfortunate Richard also saw action at the Battle of Jutland but had the good fortune to escape unscathed. Hedley Mundy, also from Landewednack, was well experienced in naval life well before the outbreak of hostilities in 1914. A member of one of the several Mundy families scattered among the St Keverne and Kynance communities on the Lizard peninsular, he had quit the family blacksmithing business to enlist in the Royal Navy at Devonport on 26 January 1906.

No doubt due to his blacksmithing skills, he started out as a mechanic and stoker 2nd class and after initial training was posted to HMS *Devonshire* as stoker 1st class with his character assessed as 'very good'. By March 1910 he had risen to leading stoker and then to acting stoker petty officer and seen seagoing service on the *Indus, Thercus* and *Gibraltar* as well as more time on the *Devonshire*. When the 1911 census was taken, he was a full petty officer aboard the second class protected cruiser HMS *Challenger* patrolling the South Pacific somewhere off the coast of Chile during a tour of China and the East Indies.

All but one of the ship's 443 crew were British. The odd man out was their commander, Captain Guy Gaunt, an Australian.

In late 1913, Hedley took advantage of shore leave to return to Cornwall and, on 13 October at St Keverne, married Bessie Jane Jose, part of the same Jose clan to which Mary Ann Sidonia Jose belonged. It was one more link from Cornwall through to my Welsh heritage.

By the time war broke out Hedley had risen to the rank of acting mechanic and, within a few months, to fully-fledged mechanic. He was now aboard HMS *Orion,* the lead ship of her class of four dreadnought battleships built for the Royal Navy in the early 1910s and which spent the bulk of her career assigned to the Home and Grand Fleets as a flagship.

This by no means implied the *Orion* sat on the fringes, her crew watching battles from the wings. There was no shortage of action for Hedley to experience.

With war looming, between 17 and 20 July 1914, *Orion* took part in a test mobilisation and fleet review. On 25 July, she was ordered to proceed with the rest of the Home Fleet to Scapa Flow to safeguard the fleet from a possible surprise German attack. Following the outbreak of war in August, the Home Fleet was reorganised as the Grand Fleet and placed under the command of Admiral Sir John Jellicoe.

On 8 August, while *Orion* was towing a target for the dreadnoughts *Ajax* and *Monarch* the latter reported she had been attacked by a torpedo and the gunnery exercise was terminated. Within days, Hedley and his fellow mechanics were confronted with serious problems with *Orion's* condensers and Jellicoe ordered she be detached to the coaling base at Loch Ewe for re-tubing.

She rejoined the Grand Fleet on 9 September but repeated reports of submarines in Scapa Flow led Jellicoe to order the fleet to disperse to other bases until the defences were reinforced. On 16 October the 2nd battle squadron was sent to Loch na Keal on the western coast of Scotland then on to the northern coast of Ireland for gunnery practice. When the dreadnought *Audacious* struck a mine on the morning of 27 October the other dreadnoughts were ordered away from the area and *Orion* had to be sent to Greenock for repairs to her turbine mounts.

For Hedley and his crewmates there was no early escape from the turbulent seas and icy winds of Britain's northern waters. From Greenock they had to sail from west coast to east, around the north of Scotland, when the navy intercepted German radio traffic and learned of mid-December plans to attack the Yorkshire towns of Scarborough, Hartlepool and Whitby with fourteen dreadnoughts and eight pre-dreadnoughts. *Orion* was one of six dreadnoughts the British sent to ambush the German ships.

Early morning darkness and heavy weather saw the opposing fleets blunder into each other on 16 December. Although the Germans got the better of the initial exchange of fire, severely damaging several British destroyers, their fleet commander ordered his ships to turn away, fearing a massed attack by British destroyers in the dawn's light. As a result of communication errors, the *Orion* failed to engage with the light cruiser SMS *Stralsund* when seen by its lookouts because her captain refused to open fire without orders from higher up the line.

He was immediately replaced by Rear Admiral Arthur Leveson and the *Orion* returned to the Orkney and Shetland Isles for gunnery drills from 10 to 13 January 1915. On the evening of 23 January, most of the Grand Fleet sailed in support of Beatty's battlecruisers, but *Orion* and the rest of the fleet did not participate in the ensuing Battle of Dogger Bank.

This was the start of several weeks of routine drills, exercises and patrols for Hedley and his shipmates. There were training manoeuvres in the northern North Sea from 7 to 10 March, and again a week later. After patrols in the central North Sea on 14 April and on 17 to 19 April, followed by gunnery drills off the Shetlands on 20–21 April, *Orion* returned to Devonport for a brief refit in late April.

More sweeps into the central North Sea occurred throughout May and the lull in action continued for the rest of the years and into 1916 with most of the time at sea spent on gunnery drills, patrols and training exercises.

Below decks Hedley heard many mutterings about the routine, even boredom, that had replaced the early days of tension and excitement.

'This ain't war, it's a bloody cruise,' he heard one rating say.

'Be careful what you wish for,' countered Hedley. 'There's lots of good men who wish they'd had it as quiet as us.'

There was no argument with this; everyone had heard the stories – some true, others mere rumour and scuttlebutt – about ships being ripped apart by the German fleet, of horrific injuries and lingering deaths when explosions had thrown men into the icy seas to float away and drown.

The patrols and drills continued into February and March but at times had to be abandoned; the continuous gales were too fierce for the escorting destroyers to contend with. Then, when the weather abated, the routine and endless drills came to a sudden stop. Hedley and his mates got the action they had been craving - even more than they had ever imagined – when the *Orion* joined the British fleet at Jutland for the massive and momentous 36-hour battle that was to become the greatest naval encounter in history.

On 31 May, under the command of Captain Oliver Backhouse, *Orion* was the lead ship of the 2nd Division of the second battle squadron and fifth from the head of the battle line. During the first stage of the encounter, her guns fired four salvos of armour-piercing shells at the battleship SMS *Markgraf*, knocking out a 15-centimetre gun and killing or disabling its crew. She next engaged the battlecruiser SMS *Lützow* at a range of

19,500 yards with six salvos and claimed to straddle her with the last two salvos that were fired at the destroyer SMS *G38* which was screening the battlecruiser and laying a smoke screen.

The *Lützow* was also fired at by *Monarch* and suffered a total of five hits from the two British ships. They knocked out two of her main guns, temporarily cut off the power to the sternmost turret and caused extensive flooding.

This was the last time that *Orion* fired her guns during the battle, having expended a total of fifty-one 13.5-inch APC shells.

Hedley had survived the only major battle of the war to be fought at sea. One in which 6,784 British sailors (including his relative, Richard Jose) lost their lives and the Royal Navy saw fourteen of its ships destroyed. German losses were 3,039 men and eleven ships.

He saw out the rest of the war on board *Orion*, becoming a certified diver and gaining steady promotion. The *Orion* served as the flagship for Rear Admiral Sir Douglas Nicholson of the Home Fleet's third battle squadron until the squadron was disbanded on 1 November 1920 and *Orion* was transferred, together with her sister ships. to the Reserve Fleet at Portland.

After nine months at shore base HMS *Vivid* in Devonport, Hedley spent two extensive postings back at sea, first on board the relatively new battleship HMS *Resolution* and then on HMS *Eagle*, now with the rank of chief mechanic.

The *Eagle* was originally laid down before the war as a battleship ordered for the Chilean navy and in early 1918 was bought by Britain for conversion to an aircraft carrier. Hedley joined her when she was recommissioned in 1924 and initially assigned to the Mediterranean Fleet.

Hedley returned to shore duties at HMS *Vivid* in October 1926. He had qualified for a war gratuity and retired with a pension on 23 January 1928 and transferred to the Fleet Reserve.

Eleven years on and at the outbreak of the next world war, Hedley had returned to the Lizard where he was working as a serpentine polisher. The 1939 Register records him as living at a serpentine shop in Landewednack, as if that was his home, and Bessie, described as a shop-holder (did she own the shop where Hedley was living?) and serpentine polisher was a patient at St Michael's Hospital in Hayle.

Whether this was a long-term stay or merely for a passing illness or injury is so far unknown. She died on 3 April 1947 at Tranquilla, the family home which still sits on the edge of the village square in Landewednack.

Hedley waited a few years before marrying widow Brenda Ann Kent in January 1953. Their time together was fairly brief as Hedley died at Helston Cottage Hospital, age 75, on 30 July 1961.

He bequeathed to widow Brenda effects with the considerable value of almost £20,000 and which hints at all manner of family divisions as Bessie, when she died in 1947, had left a mere £85, and not a penny of it to Hedley.

The mysterious Brenda also shows up in records as having been known as Brenda Ann Kent, Brenda Ann Lovat and Brenda Ann Clayton, which was her married name when living, without any mention of a husband, in Aylesbury, Bucks, in 1939. All of which goes to show the total tangle that frequently confront family historians with no one left to guide them through the maze.

Adding to the confusion is the headstone in Landewednack Parish Church marking the grave of a Brenda Anne Clayton whose age and birth year match those of Hedley's second wife.

Another Cornish mystery waiting to be solved.

HONOURED AT LAST

Pontypridd war memorial dedication service to add Edwin Berry's name

ON A COOL, DAMP autumn morning in 2012, I gathered in the Welsh mining town of Pontypridd alongside dignitaries, representatives of the British Legion and descendants of other victims of war for a brief but emotionally draining service to mark and celebrate the name of great-uncle Edwin Berry being added to the town's impressive war memorial.

For almost a century he had gone unmarked, unknown and unhonoured in this place that had been home to him, his wife and their two sons before, like thousands of others, he had marched off to serve his country. Eventually, he had paid the ultimate price, killed on the infamous Flanders Fields and with scarcely a mention in his commander's daily diary.

In hindsight, such a sudden and harsh death looks almost inevitable as his name seems to have carried a curse from his very beginning. As recorded earlier, he was the third of the twelve children (ten boys and two girls, five dying in infancy) born to my great-grandfather Alfred Jabez Berry and his wife Anne, or Annie (nee Lloyd), to have been named Edwin. The first lived a mere eighteen days, eight of them spent suffering from agonising stomatitis. The second died aged five from meningitis. And eventually this Edwin fared little better.

He first came to notice as part of the routine compilation of the family tree as I hacked away at the tangled undergrowth it had attracted. Working my way through the children of Alfred and Annie, one date immediately stood out – a prematurely early death that occurred during those terrible war-riven years from 1914 to 1919.

Edwin was recorded as dying on 26 July 1917 on that terrible and notorious battleground that came to be known Flanders Fields. And yet, sometime earlier, when I made my first visit to 'the Land of my Fathers' and traced the places where they had lived, I found no mention of a Berry on the war memorial that overlooks the harbour at Milford Haven and stands only a few paces from the house on Hamilton Terrace where Edwin's mother, Annie (my great-grandmother) had lived with her family as a teenager.

More checking confirmed that the Edwin Berry listed on the main search sites as dying in Flanders was indeed *my* Edwin Berry. His death was a matter of public record, yet this son of Milford was not remembered on his home town's war memorial, nor was there any mention of him on the memorial across the harbour in Pembroke, where the family later lived.

I needed to know why.

Suddenly, from being one of the many basic entries on my Ancestry tree, Edwin had become 'a person of interest', as police investigators like to say. I had to discover the reason for this omission.

The first step was to learn more about his background before that fateful day in the muddy fields of France. And this threw up a further surprise – and another of those detours that family historians find frustrating and exhilarating in almost equal measure. Although he bore the name of two of his siblings who had died in infancy in Scotland, in a tenement on the banks of the Clyde, Edwin was born in Wales in the family home overlooking the waters of Milford Haven.

For generations, the Berrys had looked to the sea for their livelihood – as tidewaiters, Customs officers, coastguards, shipwrights, carpenters and joiners. As the naval dockyard at Pembroke came into being, flourished and expanded this became the focal point of their working lives.

All the menfolk became dockyard apprentices, learned their trade and attained skills that stood them in good stead all their lives. With the Admiralty as their employer they could move to wherever work was available in HM Dockyards at Chatham, Portsmouth, Plymouth and Woolwich. Or they could, as young Edwin chose, use their carpentry skills to branch out in other directions.

While his brothers bravely migrated across the border into England, Edwin remained staunchly Welsh and found work as a carpenter in the booming mining towns of the Rhonda Valley. At first, he boarded at 14 King Street, Cwmdare, with below ground rope inspector David Jones, his wife Margaret and their three young daughters. But when Margaret realised another child was on the way they had to ask Edwin to move on as they needed more room.

He found lodgings at 35 Avondale Road in Gelli, on the outskirts of Pontypridd, with coalminer Henry Allen and his family, which included their attractive young daughter Edith. The mutual attraction between the young couple was inevitable and almost immediate, no doubt helpfully fuelled by living so close together under the same roof.

In no time at all, Edith was impelled to reveal the tell-tale stirrings she was feeling in her body. And so, on 21 February 1914, seven months before the outbreak of World War I, she and Edwin were married in Pontypridd Register Office with Edwin's brother Norman on hand to act as witness.

The war was in its initial tentative stages when Emrys Aubrey Berry was born a few months later, with little thought from anyone that he and his yet unborn younger brother were destined to become two of the Great War's millions of orphans. But when Emrys' brother, Norman Allen Berry, came into the world on 1 September 1916 his father Edwin was serving as a private with the Northumberland Fusiliers in France and never saw his wife or sons again.

My initial search for a date of death had produced the shock of finding the stark annotation that he was 'killed in action' and had been awarded a couple of the basic campaign medals. Scant recognition it seemed. There was nothing to explain what happened to Edwin on that fateful day in Flanders in July 1917. Whether his death was painful and lingering or blessedly sudden I would never know. All I had was that brutally brief official announcement, 'killed in action'.

Further probing took me to be website titled UK Record of Soldiers Who Died in The Great War. From there it was a simple step to the site of the Commonwealth War Graves Commission where I was quickly confronted with a picture of Edwin's headstone in the beautifully maintained Guemappe British Cemetery in the French village of Fancourt about five miles out of Arras. It was an emotional moment.

I subscribed for a print of this picture and it now sits in a frame atop my bookshelf, a daily reminder of Edwin and his sacrifice. But this was only the beginning of the saga of this battlefield death. I now wanted to know more.

As mentioned earlier, it had been a surprise and huge disappointment to find that great-uncle Private Edwin Berry, 291979, Northumberland Fusiliers, a son of Milford Haven, was not among the names on the town's war memorial. Somewhat ironically this is situated in Hamilton Terrace, overlooking the marina and estuary and directly across the road from the family home of great-grandmother Annie Lloyd when being courted by my great-grandfather (Edwin's father), Alfred Jabez Berry.

It puzzled and bothered me that the town where he grew up and learned his trade failed publicly to recognise his sacrifice even though, as I also discovered, his death and service are recorded on a website dedicated to all the men of Wales killed in war.

Another website, listing all Welsh war memorials, states that the Milford memorial commemorates 239 men who lost their lives in WW1: eighty-three from the Army and Royal Air Force, and 156 men of the naval forces, including one Victoria Cross winner. Included in the biographies of those commemorated I found that of great-uncle Edwin, accompanied by the puzzling comment, 'Edwin is not commemorated locally', and no further details.

The obvious explanation was that his adopted town of Pontypridd, where he had been worker, husband and father, had chosen to honour him instead.

True to what should be the motto of family historians everywhere – Persistence Pays – I turned to the Pontypridd Museum and discovered that only now, almost a hundred years on from the outbreak of

World War I, the town council had decided to erect a war memorial in a local park. A roll of honour was being compiled naming all those from Pontypridd who lost their lives serving in the two World Wars and subsequent conflicts.

That was the good news. The bad news was that although the list comprised more than thirteen hundred names, Edwin Berry was not one of them. In addition, the deadline for receiving names had passed. The project was complete and no more names could be added. I was up against a bureaucratic brick wall of obstinacy and an insistence that rules come before common sense. Edwin was not to receive his due recognition.

I persisted. Edwin had lived in Pontypridd for several years. He married a local girl. They made their home there and raised their two sons in the town. He deserved to be honoured.

As a lifelong journalist, I knew this was a story too good to be missed and emailed the local newspaper. The headline wrote itself: Council Denies Recognition to Town War Hero, or something similar. Thanks to the enthusiasm of reporter Carys Lewis, my pursuit of a memorial to grand-uncle Edwin soon made front page news in the newspaper and online. Previously obdurate officials rushed into action.

After numerous emails, the press publicity, searching of records and validation it was agreed that Edwin did indeed merit inclusion on the honour roll. The authorities eventually confirmed Edwin's war record and his status as a local citizen and promised that his name would be added to Pontypridd's elegant and simple tribute to the fallen.

One can only imagine the atrocious conditions faced by Private Edwin Berry, 291979, Northumberland Fusiliers, and his mates as they huddled in their dugouts beneath the German bombardment. This was attrition warfare at its very worst. The summer of 1917 was unusually cold and wet. Much of the fighting was waged in the thick mud of reclaimed marshland that was swampy even without rain. The land had been churned up by heavy artillery bombardment from both sides and the occasional dry spells were never enough to lessen the sheer misery of the troops' daily grind. Even tanks became bogged in the endless mud and soldiers often drowned in it.

How often Edwin must have yearned to be back home with wife Edith, Emrys and Norman, in their small recently built 'two up two down' terraced home at 16 Llewellyn Street, Pontygwaith, only a few doors from the post office and general store.

Llewelyn Street, Edwin's home in Pontygwaith

Edwin enlisted into the army in Cardiff at the outbreak of war and was posted to the 1/7th Battalion, Northumberland Fusiliers, attached to 149 Brigade, 50th (Northumbrian) Division. The battalion was formed in August 1914 in Artillery Place, Finsbury. It landed at Le Havre on 24 July 1916 and three days later joined the 190th Brigade, 63rd (Royal Naval) Division. It served with distinction on the Western Front throughout the war.

Their engagements are a succession of names that have been permanently etched into the annals of warfare, notorious for the atrocious conditions endured and the vast number of lives lost and horrible lifelong injuries suffered. It was relentless and unforgiving. The roll call of places where Edwin saw action includes Ypres, the Somme and the battles of Flers-Courcelette, Morval and Le Transloy.

After spending a winter on the Somme, they moved north to Arras and took part in the Arras Offensive of April 1917. Then followed the first Battle of the Scarpe and the heroic capture of Wancourt Ridge. In quick succession came the second Battle of the Scarpe, and it was after this action that Edwin was killed on 26 July 1917, aged 33.

Sadly, this seems to have happened during a period of little activity compared with what had gone before and was still to come. There were spasmodic raids into each other's territory by the Allies and the Germans. Bombs were thrown and shots were fired but there were no massive shellings nor streams of soldiers going 'over the top' from their trenches and storming enemy lines.

According to the diary of Edwin's commanding officer, *in the early hours of 23 July the Germans attacked No.2 post with intention of cutting off garrison and obtaining identifications.* Two enemy soldiers managed to work around the Allies' left flank and jump into the communication trench while a second party launched a frontal bombing attack, throwing bombs over No.2 post and into the trench behind.

> *Owing to the prompt action taken by the NCO in charge, two men in the rear were killed and the second party were driven off with bombs, leaving two dead and some of the party were wounded.*

Overnight, the battalion was relieved by the 5th Northumberland Fusiliers and proceeded to the support area. From then until 28 July, the enemy remained quiet and the battalion was engaged mainly in necessary work on repairs and maintenance to the trenches, each of which had names as if part of some urban area back home.

> *One company worked on upkeep of Shikal Avenue; one company on Kestrel Avenue, one company on making Egret and forward first trench; one company on Lion Avenue making first trench.*

During this time rations were replenished, being provided to headquarters and shuffled around with Pioneer platoon and company in Curlew Avenue going to headquarters, Marliere company to Marliere Caves and the remainder to the junction of Lion Avenue and the railway. An observation post was established at Kestrel Avenue.

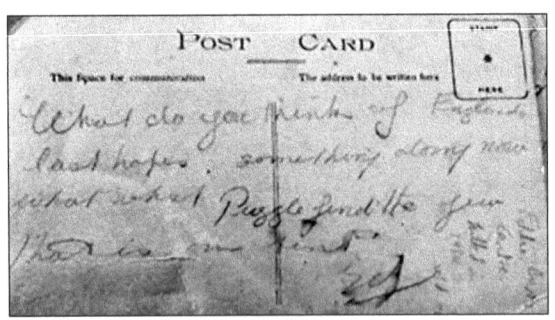

Edwin's jokey caption to the picture postcard on the next page

Ironically, it was during this fairly peaceful period of downtime and scant enemy activity that Edwin met his fate, probably from a random sniper shot as the guards were being changed.

There is no explanation of what happened other than his commanding officer's terse diary entry that simply records, *one other rank killed, one other rank injured during relief* with not even a name such as would have been attached to an officer's death. Whether his death was painful and lingering or blessedly sudden we will never know.

Beyond that, the only other information is the stark official announcement that he was 'killed in action'. That, and a simple headstone among the almost 2000 burials and commemorations of the World War contained in the Guemappe British Cemetery in the French village of Wancourt, about eight kilometres southeast of Arras. Here lies grand-uncle Edwin... and I have that framed picture of his headstone to remember him by.

According to the Register of Soldiers' Effects, all that was left for newly widowed Edith were credits of £1 9s 8d and 14s 8d (total £2 4s 4d) plus a war gratuity of £3 10s. These were approved and paid to 'Edith Berry (self and children), widow' and were not finalised until two years after her husband's death.

More than a year on from first noticing Edwin's death in action I proudly stood in Ysangharad Park, Pontypridd, to honour him in person as his name was belatedly added to his town's honour roll.

It was now some comfort to know he met his death as part of the massive push forward that culminated in the battle for Passchendaele, one of the great turning points in the thrust for an Allied victory; and I could not help feeling proud to know I had at least one ancestor among the millions of young men who died for their country.

Just one among millions but so special to me.

Such emotional links to the past show how family history can be much more than a list of names and dates. There was no more cherished moment than when my research resulted in this public honouring of a forgotten Celtic ancestor who gave his life in the service of his country.

Edwin Berry outside his tent somewhere in France

But what happened to those he left behind? Subsequent research produced only the bare facts that Edith never remarried and died in 1985 in Poole, Dorset, aged 94. As for her now two fatherless sons, Emrys died aged 60, in Hampshire in 1975, and Norman lived on into the next century, dying in 2001 in Hatfield, Hertfordshire, at the age of 84.

Nothing more could be discovered about great-uncle Edwin's family which, like millions of others, was torn apart by the so-called Great War and I was left wondering what effect this needless death might have had.

Then, in another of those surprises that make family history so exciting and rewarding, came a message from Sylvia, the only child of Edwin's brother-in-law, Albert ...

She revealed that her parents shared her childhood home in Clapham, London, with Edwin's son Emrys – always known as Aubrey – and the unmarried 'Auntie Maud'. Aubrey and Maud lived on the top floor of this Victorian terrace house while Sylvia's family, including, grandmother Elizabeth Habberfield (Edwin's mother-in-law), occupied the ground floor and basement.

Research suggests that 'Auntie Maud' was actually Edwin's widow. Much later, she moved to Poole and died there in 1985.

The families were obviously close as Sylvia's father, Albert, played a large part in the upbringing of the orphaned Emrys (more usually known by his middle name of Aubrey) and Norman.

But troubled times were ahead. Aubrey married Patricia Fitch in 1944 and they had two daughters, Valerie and Jennifer. But the marriage didn't last.

As for the girls, Val was a strong woman who brought up two sons of her own while working full-time for most of her life as a carer and also, in later years, looking after her mother. She died of ischemic heart disease in 2008 aged sixty-two. Her two boys remember happy holidays to Dymchurch with their mother and nan (Patricia). They now live in Kent with their partners and children.

Younger sister Jenny is remembered as a beauty who won the title of Miss Cliffe in the village they moved to when they left London, an achievement which made Val very proud of her little sister. Sadly, Jenny had several medical issues, including pulmonary embolism, and was continually in need of painkillers. She was only forty-six and in good spirits after having been out shopping with Val when she died in 1997.

Norman enjoyed a more successful life. He married Elizabeth Leigh and they had two sons, Graham and Adrian, who Sylvia says were very close to their grandmother, Maud. Both have gone on to be successful in their chosen careers and, like me, Graham has been in touch with the War Graves Commission for information about Edwin Berry, his grandfather.

And so the Berry name lives on in the descendants of our ancestor killed in Flanders Fields now more than a century ago.

A sideline to this branch of my Celtic tree is a fascinating story concerning Sylvia's aunt, Eva Allen, sister-in-law of my ill-fated great-uncle Edwin. Research shows she spent time in Pen-y-Val Hospital, Abergavenny, originally named the Monmouthshire Asylum in 1897 and renamed as the Monmouth Mental Hospital in 1930 before joining the National Health Service as Pen-y-Val Hospital in 1948.

The reason for Eva's stay at Pen-y-Val is given in medical records as melancholia and suicidal tendencies. Her illness was exacerbated by trauma suffered as a witness in a famous murder trial of the 1920s. Facing the judge and jury was a Major Herbert Rowse Armstrong, accused of poisoning his rich wife with arsenic and then attempting to kill a fellow solicitor.

When the family's nurse resigned because she claimed the wife was too difficult to cope with, Eva, also a nurse, had been appointed as a replacement. During the trial, the prosecution tried to turn suspicion on to Eva as having given the victim the fatal dose of arsenic that Armstrong said he had bought to use on weeds in his garden.

The trial at the Old Bailey garnered widespread attention, especially when Armstrong was likened to notorious wife-killer Dr Crippen. However, after his wife's body was exhumed, he was found guilty and hanged at Gloucester Prison on 31 May 1922.

This did little to help Eva. Not surprisingly, she suffered severe paranoia as a result of the intense cross-examination and the accusations made against her. In the 1939 Register she is described as a semi-invalid but the following year still appears in the UK and Ireland Nursing Register as holding the certificate she first gained in 1923 after earlier training at St George in the East Infirmary, London.

Eva was eventually allowed to return home from hospital to be cared for by her husband, Ernest James Young, but only after a visit to the house by a social worker who noted 'home run by husband is excellent'. Ernest was a steel mill foreman who also volunteered as an air raid warden during the war.

Ernest died in 1953 and because of Eva's incapacity, probate was handled by her brother Albert. From Albert's diaries it seems he often sent little presents of chocolates and other goodies to his sister, referring to her as 'my poor dear'.

Albert died in 1958 but Eva lived on until 1976 when she passed away in Pen-y-Val Hospital aged eighty-two.

The case, and Eva's role in it, is explained in detail in *Murders Of The Black Museum* by Gordon Honeycombe (Blake Books, 2011). There has also been a play on Radio 4 and a DVD starring Michael Kitchen as Major Armstrong. Much more recently there was a TV documentary featuring the solicitor who currently practises in the same offices as used by the major, and who is reinvestigating the murder.

A BROTHER IN ARMS

IT WAS A BETTER war - or at least a more fortunate one – for Edwin's brother Norman, four years younger than him and also born in Milford. He was still living at home at 58 Military Road, Pembroke Dock, with his now widowed father, Alfred Jabez, when war was declared in 1914. True to the family tradition, he had found work in HM Dockyard where he was steadily employed as a ship fitter and carpenter.

Although eligible for exemption, he was one of the thousands who showed no hesitation in enlisting as soon as hostilities were confirmed. On 22 September 1914, at the age of twenty-seven years and nine months he signed on for four years of military service. He was initially assigned to the Middlesex Regiment (service number 2471) and soon given the rank of acting sergeant.

From there he was transferred to the relatively new Military Provost Staff Corps with the new service number of T/1911. The MPSC was set up in 1901 to take over the staffing of military prisons all over the world that had previously been the responsibility of civilian warders. Under this new outfit, prisons were renamed detention barracks and the men were given detention barrack numbers. They ceased being called prisoners, but were soldiers under sentence, meaning they no longer had the stigma of prison attached to them.

On 18 July 1915 Norman was shipped overseas to Gallipoli – that infamous theatre of war that has become the linchpin of Australian military history, and which is the prime focus of the country's annual Anzac Day marches and commemorations.

Not only did he survive to be awarded the Victory Medal, British War Medal and the Star, but in 1919 he appears to have re-enlisted, this time in the Royal Fusiliers, although no records have yet been traced showing for how long or with what rank.

What is known is that he did eventually return to his former trade, this time at HM Dockyard, Portsmouth, where he was employed as a marine engineer until retirement. And was awarded the Merchant Service Medal.

Norman would have been one of the earlier beneficiaries of the new system of elementary education introduced across the country – a move which saw students progress from being able not only to sign their names but also to read, write and undertake the studies that led to apprenticeships and all manner of employment opportunities. Before this, such education as was available in towns such as Pembroke and Pembroke Dock – and far beyond - came either via voluntary establishments or through the National and British Schools of the Non-conformist and Anglican religions.

Formal education did not arrive in Pembroke Dock until after 1870, when Forster's Education Act created school boards whose purpose was to establish a system of elementary education across the country.

By the beginning of the twentieth century, when Norman was in his teens, government grants meant that Albion Square Board School, in the western part of the town, was offering industrial, scientific and technological education that – with the lure of a dockyard or Admiralty apprenticeship - would retain pupils beyond the normal school leaving age of fourteen.

This was not greeted with the universal approval one would have expected. There were those who felt the board, in common with many others, had exceeded its powers by offering those from the working class an education that was beyond their position and station in life. But it was an unstoppable tide that in 1902, thirteen years after the Welsh Intermediate Education Act had been passed, saw the abolishment of Pembroke and Pembroke Dock School Board.

In its place was the newly formed Joint Education Committee that rapidly established a number of intermediate schools intended to create a system that was exclusive and essentially middle class, yet offered a syllabus that combined the classics with practical subjects such as woodwork and metalwork.

In Pembroke Dock, the first such school opened in 1904. It was housed in an old hotel at the foot of the Barrack Hill and replacing the Upper Meyrick Street board school. It became known to generations of pupils as The Coro and eventually formed the foundation of Pembroke Grammar School.

Great-uncle Norman Berry was among its earliest pupils. But when a decision was made to keep the so-called Dockyard Class at Albion Square School he transferred there to complete a curriculum that would prepare him for a much-prized apprenticeship in Pembroke Dockyard.

The new system must have come as a big relief to Norman and his mates. Many of them had previously endured the ordinary board schools, with their somewhat cruel discipline meted out by masters seen as dictators of learning rather than teachers of a curriculum limited mainly to the subjects required for entrance into the Royal Naval Dockyard.

All this changed with the arrival of the new Upper Meyrick Street school's first headmaster, a Mr T R Dawes, MA, who has been described as a great success:

> ... *in cap and gown, tall and dark, with a large moustache, and spectacles hooked upon a prominent nose when they were not hanging from a double cord round his neck. He was quick in his movements and speech and gave the impression of energy and vitality. It did not take us long to discover that Mr Dawes was devastating in criticism, and had a violent temper. When he came across a careless mistake in our work he would fling our notebooks across the room, and if we began to make excuse by saying 'Please sir. I thought-' he would roll his eyes and grind his teeth in fury and almost snarl, 'Boy, who gave you permission to think?' All most humiliating. Yet he had the trick of teaching and could get the average boy through the necessary examinations.*

[From a memory by Lewis Tucker, one of the earliest pupils and who could well have been one of Norman's classmates, published in the 1949 edition of The Penvro, the magazine of Pembroke Grammar School]

This was a new era in education and Norman and his younger brother, Wilfred, were among the first to benefit. Instilled in them by these firm beginnings was a solid learning of the basics accompanied by a strong work ethic that seems to have flowed consistently through the generations that followed – no great flowerings of academic brilliance but literate, numerate, determined achievers with strong values of honesty, fairness and common sense.

MISSING AND NEVER SEEN AGAIN

Zoe Berry did not need to open the envelope the scrawny young telegram boy hurriedly thrust into her hands. She knew instinctively it contained the news every mother dreaded. The boy's frightened face was confirmation enough; he had delivered enough such messages to be aware of their contents and his look told her everything.

'Sorry, missus,' the boy mumbled and tipped his cap.

'It's not your fault, lad,' said Zoe. She handed him a penny and he scampered off, glad to be done with one more doom-laden mission.

Zoe shut the door and walked slowly back down the passage and into the shop where my Welsh cousin Edwin – Zoe's husband – was rearranging tins and packets on the grocery's shelves. He noticed the piece of paper in her hand but was slow to catch on to her slow walk and solemn look.

'What's that then, love? Has the postman been?'

Zoe held the envelope out towards Edwin. Her words were almost a whisper.

'It's one of the boys,' she said. 'You open it, I can't.' Her lips trembled and there was now a quiver in her voice. 'I know what it will say.'

Edwin, son of great-great-uncle, shipwright Joseph, and one of the few Berrys not to pursue that trade, grabbed the telegram and ripped it open. He hastily scanned the brief formal message … 'We regret to inform you …'

His hands shook as he reached out his arms and drew his wife close to him. He held her tight, trying to still her trembling body and calm her sobs. Her voice was almost inaudible.

'Which one is it?'

Edwin squeezed his eyes tight to try to stem the flow of tears; he had to stay strong.

'Cyril,' he said. He felt a shudder go through her.

'My baby boy.'

'Killed in action,' Edwin added, almost as if it mollified the blow, justified the deed, made it somehow heroic.

There was nothing more to say. They had steeled themselves for such a moment for the past two years. Every day they counted their blessings if it ended without the arrival of the dreaded telegram yet knew, with three sons away at the front, to lose one of them was almost inevitable.

The ringing of the shop's doorbell as a customer entered came almost as a relief. They broke off their embrace and wiped away their tears; life had to go on, as they knew it had for so many others up and down the country. Their loss was merely one among thousands.

Cyril Clarence Berry had been one of the first to enlist, signing up even before his two older brothers, Horace. and Percy. Britain had entered the war on 4 August 1914. Its first troops landed in France three days later and Cyril signed his 'short service' enlistment papers on 31 August. He swore he would be 'faithful and bear true allegiance to His Majesty King George the Fifth, his heirs and successors' for a term of three years 'unless the war lasts longer than three years, in which case you will be retained until the war is over'.

An optimistic handwritten note assured him if, however, the war was over in less than three years he would be discharged 'with all convenient speed'.

Cyril, an errand boy and grocery assistant in the family shop in Church Lane, Charlton, was all of nineteen years and three months old when he committed himself to joining the Middlesex Regiment as an infantryman, knowing full well that within a few weeks he would be shipped across to France to face the full force of the German army.

Like so many of the Berry line, he was slim and slight, a mere eight-and-a-half stone (53.5kg) and 5ft 5in tall and with hardly the build for carrying an infantryman's cumbersome pack and all his weaponry. Having to do this in the mud and slime of the battlefield, and while dodging endless enemy bombardments, became an enormous daily drain on his physical resources. I imagine myself – only marginally heavier and taller than this puny lad, and often castigated for being too thin – coping with what he went through, and I shudder.

Cyril encountered the full brutality of war in February 1915 when he suffered a gunshot wound to his right foot. An abscess developed and he was taken to the field hospital for treatment. He had hardly recovered from this when, four weeks later, he copped another bullet wound, this time in his right thigh and with another abscess developing. This was diagnosed as sufficiently serious to have him sent back to England for proper medical care and a reunion with his distraught family.

As her son's wounds healed and his strength returned, Zoe suffered mixed emotions.

'Sometimes I almost wish his injuries were worse,' she confided to Edwin. 'It would mean he won't have to go back to that terrible war. The better he gets the sooner we'll lose him again.'

It was the best part of a year before her fears were realised. But on Boxing Day, 1915, with General Haig now in command and the disastrous Gallipoli campaign drawing to a close, Cyril was shipped back to rejoin his mates on the front line. Within four weeks of enduring the wet and bone-chilling cold of the French winter, the abscess on his thigh had broken out again and he spent a few days in the field rest station. With the abscess spreading to his groin, Cyril was moved to hospital at Boulogne and was not thrust back into the front line again until late April 1916, weak and frail but deemed fit to fight.

The lull in fighting over the following weeks was intended to dupe the German army into a false sense of security as the British high command began planning what was intended to be a massive push through the enemy lines – the catastrophic campaign that became known as the Battle of the Somme, and the biggest list of dead and casualties in British military history.

Cyril went over the top and into the dreaded No Man's Land with thousands of other troops when the battle began on July 1. Eleven days later he was reported as missing.

One account, fairly typical of the lack of feeling shown towards the lower ranks in many of the reports and diaries, put it more brutally: 'Missing, presumed blown up'. Hardly the sort of thing a grieving mother wants to be told.

A week later it was recorded Cyril was to be regarded for official purposes as having died and a telegram was ordered to be sent to the grocery store in Church Lane, Charlton.

It was not until three years later that his mother signed a receipt for the 1914-15 Star and the Victory Medal that were all that remained of his contribution to king and country. She also received a war gratuity of £8 10s 0d.

His name, however, is commemorated in perpetuity – and 'remembered with honour' – at the Commonwealth War Graves Commission Memorial at Thiepval, France.

THE BROTHERS WHO SURVIVED

PERCIVAL EDWIN BERRY WAS not to be outdone by younger brother Cyril. Within seven days of Cyril signing on the dotted line, Percival – inevitably known as Percy – had also become an enlisted man, not in the regular army but as one of the much-derided territorials in the County of London Battalion of the London Regiment.

The regiment was first formed as a voluntary force and in 1908 merged with the Yeomanry to form the Territorial Army to regulate the various volunteer battalions in the newly formed county of London. Each battalion had a distinctive uniform and for a long while retained a measure of its original identity, independent of any regular army regiment.

Percy, however – and much to his mother's despair – went one better than Cyril by signing on for four years, not three, although this made little difference as every man who enlisted knew he would be there for the duration. This was certainly true in Percy's case; from the moment he disembarked in France from a troopship that left Southampton on March 15, 1915, he spent his entire army service on the battlefields and it was not until February 1919 that he was discharged with the customary twenty-eight days leave and a £2 advance.

In that time, this cousin and former shipping office clerk rose through the ranks from private to lance corporal then to corporal, acting sergeant and finally, in September 1918, full sergeant. His only break from the ardours of war were a couple of sojourns in hospital and two weeks leave back home in England in June 1918.

Eyebrows were raised among medical staff when Percy – as slight and slim as his younger brother – was brought into the field hospital on May 25, 1916. He had all the symptoms of an illness that was causing great debate among the doctors – a frontal headache, dizziness, severe lumbago, a feeling of stiffness down the front of the thighs and severe pains in the legs around the shin area. And, of course, there was the actual fever that had been the initial reason for his collapse.

Only a few months earlier, medical officer Major J H P Graham had recorded the admission to a casualty clearing station of a private from an infantry regiment who was suffering from 'a febrile illness of three days' duration and of sudden onset'. It was, he reported, a condition unlike anything he had previously encountered.

Army doctors and pathologists, consulting physicians and clinicians hotly reviewed and debated the growing number of cases with symptoms like those shown by Percy. The general opinion was that it was a separate and previously unrecognised disease. Its cause was variously attributed to one of the common flies or parasites found in the trenches. One likely culprit was the body louse because the disease was especially prevalent during the winter, when mosquitoes and flies were absent from the trenches. Even the common field vole or mouse was blamed, and one doctor suggested it was the result of a rat-derived infection, combined with constipation.

Regardless of the theories as to its origins, it soon earned the label of trench fever and became one of the most significant causes of sickness among the thousands of troops already suffering from the appalling conditions of life in the trenches.

'Don't worry lad, you'll be back with your mates in a few days,' the doctor assured Percy as he lay shivering yet sweating on his stretcher.

Percy was not sure whether to be comforted or dismayed by the officer's words. He wanted the fever to end but the prospect of returning to the stench and muck of the trenches was hardly a cheering prospect. But, he had his duty to do.

'How long, doc?'

'It's a new one to us, but we're finding the fever dies away within about five days. Full recovery could take up to a month and don't be surprised if it comes back to hit you again later.'

'Sounds just great,' said Percy. 'One dose of this is enough without having to face another later on.'

The doctor shrugged and moved on; there were far worse cases to deal with than a lance corporal with a fever. Percy closed his eyes and drifted off into another nightmarish sleep. As the doctor had predicted, most of the aches and sweats passed within five days but it was another nine days before he was released to rejoin his unit as they prepared for what was to become known as the Battle of the Somme – the catastrophe that was to take his younger brother's life.

Percy next saw the inside of a hospital three months later when he suffered a bayonet wound to his left hand. This was serious enough to have him removed from the field hospital to the coastal fishing port of Étaples with its notorious base camp and some sixteen military hospitals and a convalescent depot. So bad were conditions here, with up to 80,000 men in camp at any one time, that after a couple weeks many of the wounded said they would rather return to the front with unhealed wounds than remain at Étaples. In the winter before Percy's arrival, a mysterious respiratory infection had caused havoc at the base and in 1918 it was the centre of a flu pandemic or at least provided a significant precursor virus to it.

Writing in his *Collected Letters* (Oxford University Press, 1967), famed soldier poet Wilfred Owen recalled a stopover in Étaples on his way to the front:

> *I thought of the very strange look on all the faces in that camp; an incomprehensible look, which a man will never see in England; nor can it be seen in any battle but only in Étaples. It was not despair, or terror, it was more terrible than terror, for it was a blindfold look and without expression, like a dead rabbit's.*

Little wonder that in 1917 Étaples was the scene of a four-day mutiny. Soldiers took control of the camp, held violent demonstrations and disobeyed orders to stand down. It took a corps of machine-gunners to quell the uprising. Three of the mutineers were given ten-year jail sentences, a score more received lesser terms and one, Corporal Jesse Short, was sentenced to death.

Fortunately for Percy, his stay in this vast hospital city was mercifully short – just two days during which he received dressings and antibiotics for his wound before being sent back to his unit. Somehow, apart from a short bout of influenza in July 1918, he then managed to stay unscathed and relatively healthy through to the war's end. His superiors recognised his durability and leadership qualities and he rose slowly but steadily through the ranks. When he eventually arrived back at the family grocer shop in Charlton on 9 February 1919, he wore a sergeant's three stripes on his arm and fully deserved the hero's welcome he received not only from his proud parents and sister Eva – now a blossoming seventeen-year-old – but from all the neighbours.

'And just you wait until tomorrow,' said a joyful Zoe.

Percy threw his mother a puzzled look; war weary and still shell-shocked, he was already finding it hard to adjust to the sudden change. He had gone from enemy bombardments to the quiet of a suburban street in a few days; from sleeping in a blanket roll in trenches and bivouacs to slipping between sheets in a comfortable bed. He needed quiet and solitude, not sudden surprises.

'No more celebrations, please mum. Let's give it a rest.'

He made a move to escape into the back yard. She held his arm and rushed to explain.

'It's not for you. It's your brother; Horace is on his way home, too.'

Percy stopped in his tracks and a big smile lit up his face.

'There, I knew that would make you happy,' said Zoe.

She didn't know the half of it, thought Percy. His feelings went beyond happiness and relief at knowing Horace would soon be with them. It meant he would have someone to talk to who knew the full horrors of what they had both been through.

Horace had been the last of the Berry boys to sign the enlistment papers – a full nine months after Cyril, Clifford and Percy. He put his name to the forms handed to him by Company Sergeant-Major J McGregor on 26 June 1915 and, much to his surprise, was immediately drafted into the 2/7th battalion of the Gordon Highlanders.

More solid, slightly taller and heavier than his brothers, Horace was the knockabout lad of the family – the one most likely to get into scrapes and earn reprimands from teachers and superiors. He did not take easily to the rigid discipline of the army – and especially that of the redoubtable highlanders – and occasionally was deprived of his pay as penalty for his offences. Fortunately for him, these misdemeanours did not occur on the battlefield but in the comparative safety of Norfolk where the 2/7th was billeted at the army training camp at Taverham and then at the now demolished Witton Hall, once the estate of Lord Wodehouse, before being disbanded on 30 September 1918.

'It wasn't as if it was me that was hitching a ride,' grumbled Horace, back in his tent after being stopped two days' pay. 'The wagon was almost empty, and the pack was heavy. I kept on marching.'

His commanding officer, Major Simpson, had failed to share his point of view. He found Horace guilty of carrying his equipment in a transport wagon while on active service and 'when in the line of march'. It was this combination of cheek and laziness that lost him those two days' pay.

Others at Taverham committed more serious offences. It was quite common for soldiers to wander off from the tents lined up along the Fakenham Road when they heard they were to be shipped to France. One unfortunate escapee climbed into a high tree in the area known today as Ghost Hills and tied himself with a rope into the upper branches. He tied the knots so tight that he was unable to free himself and eventually died of exposure. His body remained in the tree un-noticed for many months.

'Think I'd rather take my chances against the Hun than end up like that,' said Horace when the news of the man's discovery spread through the tents.

A few weeks later he got his wish with a transfer to the 16th brigade of the Queens Royal Rifles and the 3rd Echelon, the British Expeditionary Force's administrative headquarters in France. Only now, as 1917 was drawing to a close, was Horace about to spend his days and nights hearing the endless thunder of the artillery and come face to face with the enemy.

The second battle of Passchendaele, the culminating and final attack during the third battle of Ypres, was nearing its end as the Allies fought to gain higher and drier ground before winter set in. The only way troops could be moved up to the front line was by narrow wooden boardwalks laid between the shell-holes. Slipping off the duckboards could be deadly; soldiers often drowned in mud under the weight of their equipment.

Horace had heard stories from returning soldiers and thought he knew what to expect. But nothing had prepared him for the reality. The first thing was the smell - from rotting bodies in shallow graves and from men who had not washed in weeks because there were no means of doing so; the stench from overflowing cesspits and the acrid fumes of the creosol or chloride of lime used to stave off the constant threat of disease and infection. Mingling with this was the cordite, the lingering odour of poison gas, rotting sandbags, stagnant mud, cigarette smoke and even cooking food.

Like all newcomers, Horace soon got used to the smell and found it mingling with his own body odour. He also learned to accept the presence of the thousands of rats festering the trenches. Gorging themselves on human remains and all the other detritus, they could grow to the size of a cat.

'We've got better chances against the Hun than ever beating these buggers,' said a fellow private as he and Horace dug into their mess tins for yet another feed of bully beef and beans and watched the rats scamper past. 'They breed quicker than we can kill 'em. They're killing us off faster than Jerry's bullets.'

It was no exaggeration; disease and sickness were rampant with much of it due to the rats. Lice were another huge problem and few soldiers escaped unscathed.

Horace had two brief sojourns in the field hospital in August 1918 and four days after being discharged for the second time he was back there again – this time with the same trench fever that Percy had suffered. He was too sick to be treated locally and managed a weak but grateful smile when he heard orders were being issued for him to be evacuated to England.

It meant Horace's war was as good as over. He arrived at the Western General Hospital in Cardiff on 17 September 1918 and stayed there until granted ten days leave on 6 November. By the time his leave ended, the war was over and he had to wait only until 21 February 1919 to be finally released into the arms of his welcoming family with £2 in his pocket and the specialist military qualification of signaller – a skill he never felt motivated to use again.

Like thousands of others, he went through a long and painful recovery – more mental than physical – but eventually met and married Romford woman Irene Kate Hart. They made their home in Bromley, Kent, where Horace settled into regular work as a local government clerk in the borough engineer's department. But when retirement came he was lured, as so many of the Berrys seem to be, to the coast and to the Sussex yachting haven of Chichester. He later became a resident of Aldingbourne House, now a National Heritage Listed property but then being partly used by West Sussex County Council as a tuberculosis sanatorium. He died there, age 70, on 6 October 1968, from bronchopneumonia and chronic bronchitis and emphysema.

Widow Irene lived on in their home at 9 Seafield Close, East Wittering, until her death in October 1989 at the age of 84.

Clifford Charles, the youngest of Edwin and Zoe Berry's four sons, was a mere lad of fifteen tender years when war was declared, and still only twenty when news of the Armistice was brought to him and his mates in the trenches around Ypres.

The fields of France and Belgium were the second battlefield Clifford experienced during his time as a private with the Duke of Cambridge's Own Middlesex Regiment. Earlier he had endured the heat, sand, flies and malnutrition of the Dardanelles campaign.

Like thousands of others, he received the obligatory British War Medal and Victory Medal, small recompense for the German gas attack he suffered and from which he never fully recovered. Family recollections suggest he was unable to work. This detail is supported by the passenger list of the liner *Albertic* when, in 1927, he accompanied his sister, Eva, on a voyage to Canada for a brief visit to her friend, Elizabeth Searle, in New Brunswick. Although his occupation is recorded as 'none', he did find work as a shipping clerk after his return from Canada.

Now in his late twenties, Clifford – described as 'very musical'– became engaged to 'a nice girl' but the gas took its toll before they could marry, and he passed away at the family home in Greenwich in December 1930. The cause of death said it all: pneumothorax – 'the presence of air or gas in the cavity between the lungs and the chest wall, causing collapse of the lung' – and pulmonary tuberculosis, a bacterial infection of the lungs. The war had claimed another victim.

Two years later, brother Percy also succumbed to war's insidious effects after being confined to a sanatorium in Guildford with a disease of the lymph glands. He left a widow, Elsie May (Dallimore) and £242.

With Horace the only one of their four sons still surviving, Edwin and Zoe retired from their grocery store and swapped commercial life in London's docklands for the sea breezes and gentler pace of a home on the Devonshire coast at Dawlish. They had nothing left to give.

Eva married Robert Saunders in the summer of 1932 and in late 1935 gave birth to Barry, who, so the stories go, later became somewhat disliked by the wider family as they considered him a very spoilt child.

Eva and Barry were living with her parents in Dawlish at the time of the 1939 Register, but there is no mention of husband Robert. Another mystery still waiting to be solved.

A LATE FLOWERING THAT KEEPS GROWING

FOR SOME TIME AFTER becoming aware of another link between Wales and Cornwall, I treated it as a one-off. It was a small twig on an already substantial tree and thus could be left for later pruning or, as twigs tend to do, to simply wither and drop away. Not something of great concern or interest.

But, as a result of Welsh lighthouseman Charles Nicholas's marriage to Cornish lass Sidonia Jose, the Berrys were now linked not only to the extensive Jose clan but also, through them, to several other families deeply entrenched in the tight-knit communities of the Lizard peninsular.

Thus I became ensnared in the trap that often awaits the enthusiastic family historian. Suddenly I was haring off down another long and winding track, chasing the lure and being led far from the main road.

Soon I was enmeshed in the births, marriages and deaths of names such as Morrish, Tripp (or is it Tripconey or Tripcony as various document have it?), Gilbert, Dingle, Mundy, Harris, Champion and many others. All born, raised and buried within a few miles of each other. The twig had fallen to the ground and seeded its own flourishing tree.

From this detour I gathered into the Berry fold a host of people who, in many cases, are quite distant relatives unlikely to consider us as one of their own. But that is family history for you, and I know I am far from alone in allowing my tree to run riot.

So, within these pages at least, there has to be some judicial pruning. A summary of the main branches (and a selection of the highlights) must suffice to confirm my Cornish links; further extensions of these cousins, in-laws, grand-aunts, often several times removed, can be left for others to research.

Many of the places where these ancestors lived remain little changed from a hundred years or more ago. Chief among them is Green Cottage, the place I like to consider as the family home. It is still a dominant residence among those overlooking the Landewednack village green, which unfortunately is now something of a misnomer as it has become little more than an unloved and mostly ungrassed parking lot; dusty in summer, a muddy mire in winter.

A close neighbour is Tranquilla, a house of similar two-storey design and also with a view over the green but, on my last visit, seeming somewhat rundown and in need of a bit of TLC. Both houses feature prominently in the lives of those mentioned in these pages and other ancestors I have omitted to mention.

Tranquilla, The Lizard April 2018

All Cornish connections so far related in this memoir flow out from Sidonia Jose, who married my Welsh cousin Charles Nicholas when he was tending lighthouses around the Cornish coast.

The lives of their three children who survived into adulthood have already featured in earlier pages. There is Percy who struggled to make a success of life in America; instrument maker Frances who moved to Woolwich (where some of the Welsh Berrys also lived) and married the girl next door to where he was lodging; and Elaine, who moved from her grandparents' house in Mullion to her father's family home in Pembrokeshire. There she married Post Office worker Ernest Ranner, eventually moving to Hertfordshire to be close to her parents when Charles Nicholas returned from his long sojourn in Hong Kong.

The Ranners' daughter, Elaine Lyn Sidonia, married William Lindsay and gave birth to Heather. And it was largely through Heather that I learned of the existence and eventually the extent of my Cornish-Welsh heritage. For more than a decade of email exchanges across the miles her precise and dedicated research has guided and frequently corrected me on our journey through a shared ancestry that goes all the way back to tidewaiter John Berry.

Our long-range relationship was recently further validated through DNA tests that have revealed numerous other cousins around the world.

Heather's friendship and her willingness to share her treasure trove of diaries, oral history, letters and photos have contributed greatly to the discovery and unravelling of my Celtic ancestry; a fine example of the sharing and helping that is so essential if family history is to have any real value or meaning – or accuracy.

One of the 'twigs' encountered when trawling through the previously mentioned Hedley Mundy's life was William John Mundy. He was born on Boxing Day 1888, the youngest of Hedley's two male siblings (he also had four sisters).

After leaving school in the early 1900s, William John tried his hand in the family blacksmithing business but soon decided, like Hedley, that a life spent working hammering away at red hot metal was not for him and early in 1910 made his way to Truro to find more genteel employment as an assistant in the gents' outfitting department of leading department store N Gill & Sons.

What sparked my interest, and a sense of connection to William John, was that he found lodgings in a neat and charming terrace house a short stroll from my Truro apartment. It is a dwelling I have long hankered after. It nestles between the grand pile of Truro Methodist Church and the even grander Truro Cathedral. Situated at the entrance to Union Place, now a vehicular cul-de-sac, its bright yellow walls offer an appealing and warming glow, especially when the weather is at its bleakest. It remains in at least as good a state of repair and upkeep as it would have been when William lived there a hundred years earlier.

Union Place, Truro, William's lodging place in the shadow of the cathedral

William's fellow lodger was another young man, drapery assistant William Leonard Bray from Redruth. Their landladies were elderly spinsters Mary Jane Michell and Emily Michell, who worked from home as seamstresses. Clearly a household more refined than the one William had left behind at the Lizard.

For William, however, it was merely a staging post.

On 21 February 1910 he had signed on for four years as a territorial in the Royal Garrison Artillery and twice attended training camps. But little more than a year later he resigned. The reason, as shown on his discharge papers, is blunt: *Going overseas.*

He almost immediately sailed for the United States, found work with outfitters Moskin Bros in New York but soon moved to Bay City, Michigan, and married stenographer Grace Mae Chynoweth in Houghton, on 14 August 1917.

Although Grace was born in the US, her surname suggests a Cornish heritage and maybe William's departure for the States was not as spur of the moment as it first appeared. Grace's father, James, a miner, was also born in Michigan. It is his father, Richard, also a miner, who confirms the link with Cornwall; he was born in Tywardreath and started this American line of the Chynoweths when he migrated sometime in the early 1800s.

Their family wheel turned full circle a hundred years later when Grace made her first of two visits to Cornwall. On the Fourth of July in 1923, she sailed from New York on the *St Paul* with William and son Robert (born in 1918) for William to introduce her to 'the folks back home' in the tiny fishing village of Coverack, perched on the edge of the Lizard peninsula.

It was a sad homecoming for William. His father, John, had died two years before his visit. Fortunately his mother, Mary Jane (nee Richards) was still alive and surrounded by the several members of her family who had not followed William to the US or and Bertie to Canada (in 1913).

William, Grace and Robert's visit lasted eight weeks before returning to the US on the *Homeric*. It would be nice to think this was long enough for them to include an excursion to Lanescot, the village near St Austell that was once a thriving copper mining community, to seek out any Chynoweth relatives of Grace's grandfather, Richard, and his father, another Richard.

Lanescot, recorded in the Domesday Book as Lisnestoch, grew from being the very rural manorial estate of Robert, Count of Mortain, into the home for some 1800 miners and their families, the Chynoweths among them, living along the Tywardreath Highway out to the St Blazey Bridge.

The Lanescot Mine opened in 1836, had seven large engines and thirteen waterwheels driven by water brought from Molinnis Moors, more than four miles to the northwest, by a leat and an aqueduct at Lux-ulyan. At one stage it was the third greatest copper mine in Cornwall but by 1867 all operations had ceased.

Aqueduct in the Luxulyan Valley, Cornwall, that brought water to the Lanescot mine

This sounded the death knell for the community and persuaded the Chynoweths and many of their workmates to sell their skills in mines around the world, many of them making their way across the Atlantic to begin life anew in the booming US.

Thus did the granddaughter of a Cornish copper miner marry the son of a Cornish blacksmith and returned 'home' to reconnect with their ancestral roots.

William and Grace made at least one more visit, in July 1958, when the passenger list for Cunard Line's *Ivernia* showed they were not only travelling first class, but also that William was now a fully-fledged church minister after years of studying and working as a lay preacher.

Although they stated they were visiting St Keverne, William's home on the Lizard, they gave the immigration people an address in Old Coach Road, Playing Place, on the outskirts of Truro as their temporary base. This was their last contact with Cornwall – coincidentally a very short walk from my own sister's current home. Small world, as the saying goes.

Grace died eight years later on 31 October 1966. William survived until 3 September 1979, three months short of his 91st birthday, the Cornish tailor's assistant who worked his way through storemen, shopkeeper and care worker eventually to take the cloth and leave behind another William John Mundy to carry on the family name on the far side of the ocean that batters his Lizard birthplace.

THEY CALLED HER MIMI

AND THEN THERE WAS Mimi ... and through her another link to my third ancestral Celtic nation, the Scots.

The name itself sufficed to cause tremors in this then young man's mind. It was so exotic, so far from the Mabels, Joans, Brendas, Marjories, Sylvias and Dorothys who represented the mainstay of my early contacts with the female gender.

It was also, as I discovered much later, an adopted adornment; her birth name was as prosaic as all the other women of my acquaintance. When baptised after her birth to an Irish father (Joseph Yates) and a Scottish mother (Flora, nee Barr) in the Medway town of Gillingham in July 1904 she was named Agnes Yates. But to me and many others she was always Mimi.

There was something about the way her name was uttered. It was rarely spoken in normal tones but in whispers. With it came sideways glances as if referring to an SOE operative about to be dropped behind enemy lines; or more likely, as I now realise, to some flighty dame who failed to conform to the rigid behaviour patterns of our rather staid middle class life.

This air of mystery was further enhanced in those less worldly times by the places connected with her name; lands and cities discovered by turning the globe during geography lessons or studying the postage stamps being diligently gummed into a Stanley Gibbons album.

She seemed to float in and out of our lives, never less than exquisitely attired and always somehow recently arrived from or on her way to yet another faraway location to be searched for in the atlas.

The vision has always been of someone tall, slim and willowy, wrapped in a swathe of colourful gowns that billowed in her wake; a being as remote from the glum, grey gloom of postwar Britain as was Mars from Margate, where weekend excursions were spent on the pebbly shore wishfully described as a beach.

Mimi's precise relationship to our small family unit was never defined, or at least not that I can recall. It was only in recent times that I confirmed she was a much closer relative than I ever realised at the time thanks to her being referred to as from 'the other side' – an indication she was connected more to my uncles and aunts, rather than having a direct link to either mum or dad and hence to me. Yet she was always considered as family, regardless of how random or infrequent her appearances might be.

I had a vague awareness of Mimi having more than one husband – maybe several – but such multiple liaisons were not something talked of in those strait-laced days, at least not in front of the children. I also recollected mentions of voyages to and from the West Indies, of wartime seclusion in the Argentine and later settling in South Africa. But I had no idea of where this dovetailed in with my more mundane relatives and, specifically, with my jolly, homely Auntie Floss and her husband, the ever-jocular Uncle Syd, my dad's elder brother.

It was only much later that I learned that Mimi was the younger sister of Floss and hence another aunt. But even today a more unlikely pairing of sisters remains beyond imagining.

Auntie Floss – shown on her birth certificate as Flora Barr Yates – was the epitome of homeliness, an unruffled do-anything-for-anybody mother figure. Always jolly and jovial. Mimi was exotic, sparky, madcap even. Or, as first cousin June Berry – daughter of Floss and Syd – informed me during the writing of this book, 'a fling-over-the-traces sort of person who inevitably married too quickly'.

And married again, and again. First to a Welsh engineer – that Celtic link again – who took her off to the West Indies, and then to a handsome Argentine naval officer Alfred Cassels who took her dining with the captain of the *Graf Spee* and to live in Uruguay during the war. After nursing Alfred through to his death from cancer, she returned to London, before meeting Presbyterian minister Roland Vipont and eventually ending up in South Africa.

My abiding memory of Mimi is, when as a gauche teenager, I received this still grieving widow's invitation to join her for lunch in London. Today's teenagers would probably mutter 'whatever', decide if they could be bothered to accept and see little cause for excitement.

But in postwar Britain, a restaurant meal was a rare event. It was the preserve of the privileged and well-to-do, not something experienced or even considered by a mere child. Eating was for survival and sustenance, not for pleasure. Dining-out as a pastime was still decades away, as unimaginable as the subsequent advent of foodies, celebrity chefs, cooking shows, cookery books as bestsellers and the mass fascination with the preparation, presentation and consumption of food for enjoyment.

And here was I, awkward and unworldly, taking the train from Gillingham to London for a lunch date with a beautiful and exotic woman. Even more daunting, the venue was not the nation's then culinary mainstay, a Lyon's Corner House or its High Street lesser lights, but a far more refined eatery in the heart of Mayfair.

The experience left me dumbfounded and impressed in equal measure and has remained so down all the decades since.

Yet it was only many years later, when food became a fascinating and dominant feature in my life, that I realised how much of a treat the delightful Mimi had bestowed on me. We were dining at the pinnacle of what little fine dining existed in Britain in those austere postwar days of shortages (who won this war, anyway?) and food rationing.

Mimi worked at the Cordon Bleu School of Cooking set up by Rosemary Hume and Constance Spry. Hume was a graduate of the original Paris-based Cordon Bleu Cookery School. Spry, a famed florist and interior design expert, had reigned supreme since the 1920s over the floral arrangements and hostessing needs of British society.

Pre-war, Spry organised the flowers for the wedding of the Duke of Windsor and Wallis Simpson and went on in 1953 to manage the flower arrangements at Westminster Abbey and along the processional route for the coronation of Queen Elizabeth II.

She and Hume were also credited with inventing the still popular dish known as coronation chicken when they were preparing the food for the Queen's wedding banquet.

It was in this rarefied atmosphere that I had my first encounter with food elevated to the status of a craft. Here, amid Spry's wondrous floral designs, it was presented for sensory pleasure; as theatre to be savoured, rather than as a mere necessity to be gulped down and forgotten.

Long before Jamie, Delia, Nigella and Co there was the Constance Spry Cookbook

Fading memory has wiped away all details of what we ate, yet the impact of that occasion has remained. I credit Mimi with the early awakening of my lifelong fascination with cooking and dining. Maybe it is a step too far to suggest she saw something in me that needed to be stirred into life. But I like to think that is the case and remain forever grateful.

It is also through her, along with Auntie Floss and their brothers Joe, Stanley and Victor, that I can make further claims to my third Celtic link. Their mother, also called Flora (Moodie), was born in Scotland, in Lanarkshire; as was her mother, another Flora (Anderson), born in Glasgow; and her mother, again called Flora (Rankin) and born in Glasgow.

And adding a lovely touch of synchronicity, Auntie Floss's mother and grandmother at one stage lived in the hard-grind area of Glasgow known as Govan, which is where – as already explained – my direct Welsh forebears briefly migrated in the late nineteenth century.

Govan was also where my grandfather, Alfred Berkeley Berry, great-uncle Hugh and great-aunt Elizabeth were born before the family returned home to Wales – Scots on their birth certificates but thoroughly Welsh for all but a few infant years.

Celts through and through.

TRAGEDY AT THE LIGHTHOUSE

As far back as I have been able to delve, the patriarchal side of my Celtic family has always had close links to the sea. Most have lived in coastal towns and villages around the nation. In keeping with its ever-fluctuating nature, the tide's ebb and flow has provided our menfolk with the gamut of life's ups and downs. It has brought them employment, skills and opportunities. On the downside there has been uncertainty, hardship and sudden death, in peace as well as in war.

They have served the sea as shipwrights, blacksmiths, mariners, tide-waiters, missionaries, lighthouse keepers, fishermen, Customs officers, gunners, stokers and deckhands. Their homes have rarely been more than a brisk walk from the shipyards, docks, wharves and moorings where they worked.

Even those who broke the mould and pursued other trades did so in places washed by oceans and rivers. And from such photos as I have been able to source from the past, it seems their leisure hours were also spent by the sea rather than in the country.

My own life – although professionally devoid of any maritime connections – has mirrored those of my ancestors; living always closely within sound and smell of the water with sailing, kayaking and swimming high on my list of activities when younger. To say one has the sea in the blood may sound cliched but when pushing through the foliage of our family tree it is something hard to deny about the Berry male line.

Not even those who made careers seemingly unconnected with the sea could escape its influence on our lives. No better, nor more tragic, example of this was my great-great-grandfather Hugh Brown. Although he and his family lived in Oreston, this ancient boating community abutting Plymouth nestles so close to the border with Cornwall that his inclusion among my Celtic kinfolk needs little justification.

Added to which Plymouth is among the most solid of seafaring cities with a maritime history going back way beyond the days of Drake, the Armada, Sir Walter Raleigh and the Pilgrim Fathers. And it is where my Welsh grandfather, Alfred Berkeley Berry, lived and worked and where my father was born, within a rivet's echo of the naval dockyards.

Perhaps Hugh should have seen all these connections as an omen – a reminder that, for better or for worse, many of my family's menfolk are inevitably embroiled with the sea. Although he worked as a stonemason, that would provide no escape from the sea. After all, it was Oreston artisans who helped build the first lighthouse to be erected on the treacherous Eddystone Rock, ten miles off the Cornish coast, at the end of the seventeenth century.

And it was to this dangerous outcrop that Hugh was sent in August 1839, some fifty years before my Welsh cousin, Charles Nicholas, tended lights off that same Cornish coast at Wolf Rock and the Lizard and married into a Cornish family.

Although the Eddystone rocks are officially in Devon they form part of a treacherous reef located nine statute miles (14 km) south of the Cornish coast at Rame Head, part of the South West Coastal Path and a Heritage Park on its own right. A place where Celtic warriors built a rampart across the headland to defend it from possible attack, and medieval monks kept a light burning to warn sailors of the rocks.

Before the building of the first Eddystone light in 1698 the reef was an ever-present danger to shipping, especially to vessels making for Plymouth. As many as fifty ships a year were wrecked and numerous lives lost.

The original tower was the first lighthouse to be built on a small rock in the open sea. It was the work of eccentric showman Henry Winstanley who had blessed Londoners with Winstanley's Waterworks near Hyde Park. For decades it was one of London's foremost popular attractions.

The lighthouse lasted only until 1703 when it was obliterated by a huge storm that took Winstanley and five of his workers with it.

A replacement survived but when this wooden structure was destroyed by fire in 1755 Yorkshireman John Smeaton decided to construct a stone tower based on the shape of an English oak tree to give it strength. He engaged a workforce of the toughest labourers, many of them former Cornish tin miners. With press ganging rife at the time, his workers were declared as exempt from being kidnapped into naval service.

Trinity House arranged with the Admiralty to have a medal struck for each labourer to prove they were working on the lighthouse. It also based its operations at Hugh's home town, Oreston, source of stone for the lighthouse and of skilled stonemasons.

Great-great-grandfather Hugh's presence on the Eddystone Rock followed a visit by government engineers into the aftermath of several recent severe storms. They reported there was no structural damage to the lighthouse but repairs were needed near the landing stage. A gap had opened up in the rocks and had to be filled in. This was the task facing Hugh and three workmates on that Thursday morning.

It was nearing midday when a wave swept in that was later described as 'much larger than could have been expected from the tranquil state of the water'.

Even though he was a strong swimmer, Hugh did not stand a chance. The wave curled up and over the space in which he was working and carried him out to sea. Life jackets, harnesses and Workplace Health and Safety did not exist. His workmates did throw a cork line to him but his heavy boots weighed him down.

As the *Plymouth Journal* brutally but almost poetically reported, 'He soon sunk to rise no more'.

He was forty-seven-years old.

Forty years after Hugh Brown worked there, it was discovered that the rocks upon which the lighthouse stood were becoming eroded and the present structure was built to replace it.

Although Smeaton's lighthouse was largely dismantled and rebuilt as a memorial on Plymouth Hoe, its foundations and a stub of the old tower remain on the Eddystone Rocks. The light may have been shaken from side to side each time a large wave hit it, its foundations

Eddystone Light profile shown in an engineer's profile

proved too strong to be dismantled. They were stronger than the rock upon which the tower was built and could not even be intentionally taken apart.

Hugh's wife Amey, my great-great-grandmother, a local girl and six years Hugh's junior, was seven months pregnant with their sixth child,

William. An already hard life suddenly became many times tougher.

Within two years she is registered in the 1841 census as a pauper, still living in Oreston with six children at home and only one, seventeen-year-old Thomas, able to bring in any money from his job as a labourer.

But Amey was a battler. She kept the family together and remained in Oreston where she had friends and family for support. By 1851, three of the children had left home; Thomas was still working as a labourer and eighteen-year-old Hugh was following in his father's footsteps as a local stonemason. Youngest child William was at school and yet to join the workforce but there was added income from a stonemason lodger, widower John Lidstone.

Ten years on and the household had shrunk to three and life had much improved. Amey was now an annuitant, William was a ship's carpenter and widower Lidstone (whose long-standing role in this domestic set-up could by now be open to conjecture) had become a blacksmith.

Amey's pauper days were long gone. She remained a widow and by 1871 was living alone in Silver Lane, Oreston, with a servant girl Ellen Brown (no family connection) to help with her failing health caused by chronic bronchitis. It was this and heart disease that caused her death on 3 February 1873.

Her youngest son, William, my great-grandfather, left home in 1861 to marry Plymouth girl Thomasine Jane Holton. They and their nine children moved to the Medway towns in Kent, another major dockyard centre.

Grandparents: Alfred Berkeley Berry and his wife Emma (Brown)

It was there that daughter Emma met and married my Welsh shipwright grandfather, Alfred Berkeley Berry, and, in 1908, gave birth to my shipwright and eventual Customs officer father ... which in turn led to our family's eventual settlement in Celtic Cornwall in yet another legendary seaport.

Sadly, this story of the Browns ends much as it began, with a sudden and unexpected death.

On 2 April 1936, when I was a mere seven months old, grandmother Emma decided to end her life. As Medway Coroner E Cecil Harris concluded at the inquest on 1 May, she placed a gas tube in her mouth 'whilst of unsound mind' and was asphyxiated by self-induced coal gas poisoning.

The whys and wherefores of such drastic action remain a mystery. All who could provide answers, and their descendants, have long departed. Much searching and requests for information have failed to uncover the coroner's report and no references have so far been found in newspapers of the time. Back in those days such events were talked about only in hushed tones and definitely not in front of the children. This guaranteed I was not privy to any hints as to the reasons behind grandma's suicide either then or at family gatherings in later years.

However, I did have cause to wonder when research confirmed that little more than a year after Emma's death Grandad Berry – known inexplicably to all as 'Bindle' – married widow Florence Tucker (nee Stone), who promptly and disrespectfully became known, although never to her face, as 'Steppy'.

And therein lies another intriguing tale lost with the passing of all involved.

A CAPTAIN'S FATAL STUMBLE

THE DEEPEST ROOTS OF my Celtic heritage are firmly lodged in the far south-west of Wales, around the magnificent vast harbour of Milford Haven and the ancient dockyard and fortress city of Pembroke.

It was therefore quite some time after this initial discovery that I found those early beginnings were followed a generation later by the sprouting of a flourishing Welsh offshoot based in Swansea, a city perched on the edge of the splendiferous Gower Peninsular – the UK's first Area of Outstanding National Beauty.

The Berrys who migrated here from around Milford also thrived, mostly by staying true to such maritime trades as shipwrights, carpenters, seamen, lighthouse keepers and engineers but also, thanks to Britain's all-round industrial progress, venturing further afield than their forebears.

It was from here that the seeds were sown of what has become an outpost of kinfolk entrenched on the US West Coast in California and a huge source of many a tale of intriguingly entangled relationships painstakingly documented and watched over by retired Sacramento University geography Professor Emeritus Bob Richardson.

Cousin Bob, as I like to think of him, has become a regular correspondent and about as close a friend as one can get across thousands of miles of ocean. He has also unstintingly made available his vast archive of documents, pictures, newspaper clippings and oral history.

Now retired, he uses his lifelong skills as an academic to dig deep and wide into the family's past, never letting information become a fact until it is thoroughly verified. As a result, we have exchanged innumerable notes comparing data that far too often is merely supposition copied from one Ancestry tree to another.

But that side of the Berry clan is very much Bob's story to tell. For now, I will stick with the true Celts on the Welsh side of 'the pond' and with the sad tale of cousin Florence Rosena Berry and her seafaring husband, William Richardson.

The main source of what became a Swansea mini-colony of Berrys was great-great-uncle John Berry who, as recorded earlier, was born in 1837 to great-great-grandfather John and wife Ann in their tiny creekside cottage in the village of Coombs.

Together with his nine siblings, John spent most of his early years in Milford Haven and learning his trade as a ship's carpenter.

In 1863, as a fully-fledged shipwright and journeyman, he married dressmaker Emily Powell and together they set up home at 76 Robert Street, Milford, next door to the Nicholas family of lighthouse keepers who were the foundation of my Cornish connections.

Within a year Emily had given birth to the first of their nine children, five girls and four boys, who made their appearance with almost clockwork regularity every three or four years. The second daughter, Florence Rosena, born in 1870, needed little urging to take up her mother's craft – *There's always work for someone who can sew a good stitch* – and, when school days were over, she developed into a skilled dressmaker able to help with the family's finances after her father's death at the age of 50 in 1887.

The family had earlier moved to 28 Nichol Street in Swansea where John had risen to become a foreman shipwright. And it was here, no doubt partly due to her father's dockside connections, that Florence met the handsome and well-travelled Welsh-born mariner Frederick William Richardson, an ancestor of cousin Bob, the Californian professor. [And, as mentioned earlier, it was this coupling that created the link between myself and cousin Amanda, the original spur to my discovery of Welsh ancestry].

Florence Rosina Berry who married fated mariner Frederick William Richardson

Frederick had obtained an early taste for sea travel when, at the age of five, his parents sailed to New York on the 2539-tonne SS *China*, the Cunard Line's first screw-propelled steamship and its first ship to carry emigrants. The Richardsons were among 753 third class passengers crammed on board along with 150 in cabin class.

[The *China* made its final sailing for Cunard from Liverpool to New York on 9 March 1878. Then followed a chequered history, registered as

Spanish and renamed *Magallanes* in 1888, converted to sail as a four-mast barque and renamed *Theodor* in 1889 before finally leaving from Tampa for Yokohama in March 1906, with a cargo of phosphates and subsequently listed as 'lost in rather strange circumstances'].

Why the family uprooted themselves from all their family ties in Wales is unclear. Any skills possessed by the father – another Frederick – were more clerical than technical; he seems unlikely to been employable as a coal miner or doing the hard yards on the goldfields of southern California, which was the final stop on their transatlantic journey.

Little more than a year after their arrival in the US, a second son, George, was born to wife Louisa (nee Worth, from Barnstaple in Devon). Another, Walter Hogben, arrived two years later but died of a fever in May 1875 at the age of 18 months. Their only daughter, Louise Sara, was born in May 1875, an event that was diminished six months later when her father, after misusing his accountancy skills, was sentenced to 10 years in San Quentin Gaol for 'embezzlement as a bookkeeper'. This was later commuted by half with he and Louisa apparently enjoying an intimate celebration of his release that resulted in son Edward John being born in March 1882, only to survive for five years.

By now eldest son Frederick had well and truly left home. Like so many of the Berry clan, the lure of coast and sea had been too strong to resist. He returned to his native Wales, to Swansea, to become a merchant seaman and be granted his 2nd Mate Certificate by the Board of Trade on 7 December 1888 at the age of twenty-one.

From there he climbed steadily through the ranks to attain the title of Master Mariner and become a popular and well-regarded figure in Swansea shipping circles.

It was a career that took him all over the world although, as he remarked in 1919 in a letter to his brother George, '*It does seem strange that of all the places I go in the world, I can never strike San Francisco or the North California Coast*'.

His seagoing life was also not without its setbacks and there were times when wife Rosena struggled to cope with his long absences and the periods when he was without a ship, even though this meant he spent more time at home with her and their two sons, their only daughter, Florence Louisa, having died in 1900 at the age of five.

World War I had a dire effect on Frederick and his family. The ship-owner he worked for sold five of its ships, leaving a fleet of four. Because the men crewing them were all senior to Frederick he was left without work. In another letter to brother George in California in March 1916, he explained, '*A couple of years ago I thought I was fixed for as long as I cared to follow the sea. One never knows what is going to happen in this old world. It is full of disappointments and I seem to have been born under an unlucky star*'.

Being laid off had hit him extra hard as he had medical fees to pay when elder son Arthur became very ill. The family also had to cope with the soaring cost of food which was now almost fifty per cent higher than before the war. Because of all this he was unable to continue an arrangement to help George with regular payments for their sick mother's medical care, '*But as soon as I get a berth I will continue them*'.

But it was never to be.

Late in 1919 Frederick returned to work with the cargo shipping company J B Sutherland, based in Newcastle. The firm also had waterside docking interests in the port of Blyth. It was here that Frederick arrived as master of the S S *Roxburgh* in December 1919. Once loading had finished for the day, Frederick and some of the crew went ashore to enjoy refreshment in one of the local pubs. A fatal mistake.

It was a foul and stormy night with the ship rising and falling on the sea swell when Frederick returned to the Roxburgh about 10 pm. As fourth engineer Joseph Martin later stated to Coroner M P M Dodds, it was also very dark and Frederick called out for the quartermasters to shine a light. This lit the only way aboard, a ladder

Frederick Wm Richardson who died in Blyth after falling from the gangplank when boarding his ship

resting almost horizontally across the six-foot gap between wharf and ship.

Frederick, wrapped in a heavy overcoat, at first attempted to walk but soon realised that was too risky and got down on all fours to crawl his way across. After only four rungs he swayed, lost his grip and toppled sideways to plunge into the murky, icy water.

Heroically, engineer Martin dived in after his captain and searched around for five bone-chilling minutes. Without success.

Chief mate Frederick Arrowsmith was roused from his bed and took a while to understand the hubbub that was going on. When he looked over the ship's side he saw someone in the water and lowered himself by rope into a dinghy that had come alongside.

'We skulled around for about fifteen minutes and then I went up on to the staithes (wharf) to see if I could see anything in the water. My attention was drawn to the deceased floating in the water and I called for a doctor.'

Other crew members recovered Frederick's body no more than twenty minutes later. Artificial respiration was tried, without success.

'He was quite dead,' Martin sombrely told next day's inquest. 'I think he caught his foot in his overcoat that got in the way.'

Mate Arrowsmith told the coroner that normally the ship would have been boarded via gangways and admitted it would have been 'very much better' if one had been in place on this occasion. But it was not practicable to use them because of the state of the weather and the movement of the ship.

Inevitably the question arises of whether drink played a part in this dockside tragedy. Engineer Martin said Frederick sank four or five whiskies while he was with him but had no idea if he had been drinking before they met up. However, he assured the coroner that Frederick was able to 'walk quite steady' as they made their way back to the chip.

Thus a verdict of accidental death was recorded. This was no consolation to distraught wife Rosena, alone at home at 22 Windsor Terrace, Swansea, with both sons now far away. In a letter to George Richardson in California informing him of his brother's death, Rosena's niece, Beatrice Thomas, said her aunt was 'too ill to write' but had received a letter from the ship's owner stating how highly respected and esteemed Frederick had been by all who knew him.

The funeral and interment, a men-only affair, took place at St Gabriel's Church, Swansea, with several of the Berry family, four of Rosena's brothers and two her nephews, among the chief mourners.

One more sad outcome of the turbulent love affair my Celtic kinfolk have always had with the coast and the sea.

FUNERALS AND BIBLES

FUNERALS ARE CERTAINLY NO funfest, although there is a welcome modern tendency to attempt to lighten the mood and make them more of a celebration than has traditionally been the case; a send-off without the dark and dreary garb and often fake mournful faces, a happy cheerio with colour, gaiety and lively music such as the dear departed once revelled in.

It is a constant irritation to think that any such occasion that must eventually be held in my name will proceed without my active participation beyond being a body in a box or, preferably, a wicker basket. What is the point of a party in which the guest of honour – and the one who foots the gargantuan bill – cannot take part? I will attend only with great reluctance and protesting to the last.

However, from the narrow point of view of the family historian, funerals can provide a rich lode from which to mine hitherto hidden information. Distant, even previously unknown, relatives emerge from the woodwork, willing to reminisce, often in quite vivid detail.

Thus it was when I travelled to Southport – on the coast, naturally – for the beautifully low-key farewell to cousin Joan Berry, the larger than life eldest daughter of Uncle Syd (my father's brother) and Auntie Floss.

With a nine-year gap in our ages, which seems a chasm when young, Joan is another of the inner family circle remembered more as legend than reality; our paths obviously frequently crossed but the age difference created a void too wide for social connection. Any recollection I have of her thus depends on tales and gossip rather than any personal recall; a mental picture of my own creation of a fun person with a loud jolly laugh, an adventurer and rule-breaker, who raced around the countryside on a motor-bike when such outrageous behaviour was not expected or accepted from young 'ladies', and continued to do so well into her senior years.

Like many a Berry before her, she was drawn to the coast, a competent and regular sailor and, when war came, she inevitably enlisted in the Women's Royal Naval Service (WRNS), popularly referred to as 'the Wrens'.

In July 1952, she married Birmingham-born Joseph Cade and they had two daughters, Sara and Melanie, both of who I met for the first time at the nicely joyful gathering that followed their mother's funeral service, Melanie having flown in from her home on the far west coast of Canada.

It was while catching up with these and other long lost relatives (perhaps a catchy title for a TV program; oh, sorry, too late) that I was approached by another hitherto unknown resident of the Berry family tree. And she came bearing a wonderful and totally unexpected gift.

The family bible – damaged but not beyond restoration   *A mended spine*

Second cousin Sylvia is a direct descendant of my great-aunt Elizabeth, one of the three children born to great-grandfather Alfred Jabez Berry when he and wife Annie made their brief migration to the banks of Scotland's river Clyde. Her father's ancestry is impeccably Welsh, born in Pembroke to a shipwright (what else?) from Glamorgan. One more building block in my Welsh ancestral mansion.

And somehow or other, through all the various links and the numerous shifts and changes that create (and divide) families, Sylvia had become the guardian of the family bible – a massive leather-bound doorstopper of a book that she sincerely believed was not hers rightfully to possess.

Thus it was that a few weeks later Sylvia and I travelled from our respective homes to meet again at the edge of a frozen playing field in

Bournemouth where she handed me a sturdy woven Sainsbury's shopping bag containing the Berry family bible.

'It's yours, no one has a better claim to it than you,' said Sylvia. She had done her research and was satisfied that I was the last of the line. Not only satisfied, but also relieved to have been able to pass it on.

We warmed ourselves with bowls of soup as I gently turned the fragile pages, many of them discoloured and torn with age. Its decorated cover was in sad repair and its spine broken, but it was mostly fringe damage, the wear and tear of the years as it was passed from generation to generation.

Back in Cornwall, a county with strong appeal to practitioners of traditional arts and crafts, I was able to locate a skilled bookbinder and illustrator following in the footsteps of his equally skilled father – both of them renowned for their restoration work on old books and manuscripts.

Fittingly for such an ancient craft, the Book Bindery run by Tom O'Reilly is located within the idyllic grounds of one of Cornwall's historic estates, Port Eliot, the ancestral seat of the Eliot family. Their 6000-acre domain embraces a stately home, its own church – which serves as the parish church of St Germans and was once the site of Cornwall's main cathedral – and several surrounding villages.

There could be no better surroundings for such a traditional skill as now being carried on by Tom Reilly. He took hold of my bible with all the care and gentleness expected from one immersed in this old craft. It was, he agreed, in need of much TLC, something which he would be pleased and proud to provide.

And so he did. A few weeks later I stood in Tom's tumbledown, low-roofed cottage (what else would one expect?) and choked with emotion to see the bible's leather covers restored and polished, its broken spine repaired and the many once loose pages firmly back in place. And to protect this family treasure, Tom had provided a hardboard slip case.

A beautiful solid and tangible link between my home in Cornwall to our family's beginnings in Wales.

THE END OF THE LINE

THROUGHOUT THE WRITING OF this book I have laboured against the forces of time. The longer I researched and the deeper I delved, the more the pressure increased. The detours and distractions of extended research scream out that my task is not yet finished; not by a long way.

There are other ancestors to discover, more stories to be unravelled and told. Loose ends to be tied. What you have in the preceding pages is but a snapshot of one section of the Berry family tree. So much more discovered on this excursion back down the centuries still sits unused in my files.

Family historians talk of growing a tree, a single entity, whereas it would be closer to the reality to refer to the creation of a garden into the past. Thus what is on display here is a carefully chosen selection of 'plants' specific to tracing my Celtic heritage. It is the front garden of my 'house' so to speak. Plenty of variety, neatly laid out, each plant clearly defined yet merging into the overall design. Something that hopefully will appeal to passersby, perhaps make them pause awhile, even keen to know more.

Meanwhile, the acres spreading out from the rear of the house are what Kew aficionados would likely describe as natural or freeform, even wild or untamed. It is mostly unpruned, rarely weeded and is what the majority of family trees become when allowed to grow uncontrolled and almost self-seeding.

Too many of the trees found on Ancestry and similar services lack attribution and sources. They spread by their owners grabbing twigs from other trees and grafting them on to their own without even the most basic checking. Dates are awry (children born before their parents), locations and addresses make little sense, the detail of a wife usually having a different surname from her husband is ignored, a lack of logic pervades.

Tread through such jungles with the utmost care. The traps, even for the wary, are innumerable.

Compiling this history has made me acutely cognisant that our lifespan is finite, even without allowing for the unexpected, the unforeseen and the sheer bad luck that may await us.

Now in my eighty-fourth year, clearly my use-by date has long expired. My 'three score years and ten' have turned from years in the bank to a massive overdraft. Of all the deadlines that I have worked under for much of my life, most of them daily, this is the worst; the one that truly fills me with dread and piles on the pressure.

As ever, there is a task to be completed; but now I have to ask, can be it be finished before my time runs out?

In short, I am the last direct male descendant of the Berry line which, at least in modern times, has its roots in the far west of Wales. There is therefore no one to either continue our story or to tidy up the many loose ends that I am still rushing to research and resolve.

Several close connections share these same roots but, understandably, most of those who continue to explore this shared ancestry are now following their own spreading branches and only occasionally return to the main trunk. That is the nature of family history; although we are all linked, our main interest lies in pursuing our more immediate personal heritage.

We are like a large group of ramblers setting out from their assembly point on the village green and then drifting off in ever-decreasing numbers to check on something that has caught our eye, eventually to be found wandering alone down lanes, byways, footpaths and tracks far from the signposts that indicated our original route.

But, unlike those ramblers, there is no agreed common destination; no warm and welcoming inn where we all reassemble, although our paths may occasionally merge or cross along the way.

It is a journey without a clearly defined end, a voyage into the unknown akin to those of the early explorers who sailed bravely forth not knowing what they might encounter.

This, then, has been my purely personal (some might say self-indulgent) log of one such voyage – a notebook of discoveries, facts and conjectures, of surprises and revelations, and of newly-discovered births, marriages and deaths.

Confining my research to the Celtic connections, plus the occasional fictional imagining of conversations, has meant the focus of this history has been mainly on the paternal side of the family. It was through its menfolk that for several generations the Berry line flourished and expanded until wars and the general decline in the size of the normal family unit (no doubt due to better birth control and the advent of the Pill) saw the main trunk of our tree gradually taper off until thinning out to a final fragile point.

There are two Cornish-bred nieces, one Cornish grand-niece and two Cornish grand-nephews to carry the Celtic line – but not the name – forward. My two grandsons are Australian-born and bear the name of their wholly Aussie father.

In contrast, the maternal side, has flourished. But so far as the *raison d'etre* of this history is concerned, it offers only one almost incidental Celtic connection which was via the marriage of my parents. This saw the grafting of my Devon-born Welsh father on to a tree that originated from roots deep in the Yorkshire soil and spread to the more mellow Sussex shores before helping found what is now almost a dynasty thriving in a spread of small communities in the North Island of New Zealand.

The maternal side's struggles to surmount its impoverished beginnings, hardships and setbacks have already been recorded in my earlier memoir, *From Paupers to iPads,* and thus are not repeated here.

Instead I offer a record of genealogical 'travels' that are an exploration of the deeply-felt ties that so late in life drew me relentlessly and irresistibly to two lands with a common culture yet which I had only recently experienced.

It has been a journey of affirmation, a homecoming. I am a Celt.

Over to the next generation ……

The future is in their hands

Lightning Source UK Ltd.
Milton Keynes UK
UKHW021950180719
346412UK00004B/902/P